Math

Grade **1**

AF207655

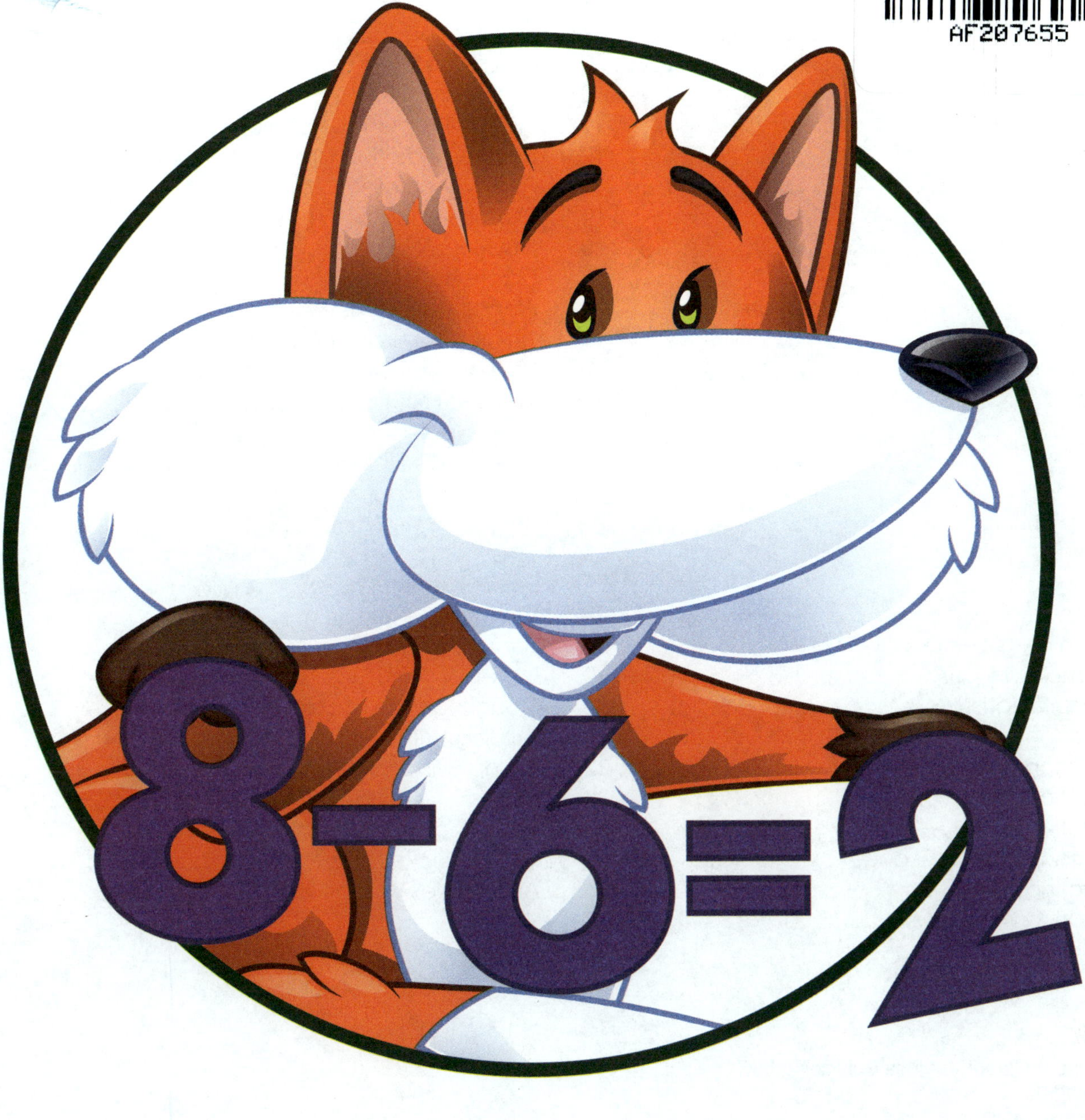

CARSON-DELLOSA™
PUBLISHING GROUP

Greensboro, NC 27425 USA

Table of Contents

Brighter Child®
An imprint of Carson-Dellosa Publishing LLC
P.O. Box 35665
Greensboro, NC 27425 USA

ISBN 978-1-4838-1652-4

01-000000000

Number Recognition 1, 2, 3, 4, 5

Directions: Use the color codes to color the parrot.

Color: 1 = red, 2 = blue, 3 = yellow, 4 = green, 5 = orange

Number Recognition 6, 7, 8, 9, 10

Directions: Use the color codes to color the carousel horse.
Color: 6 = **purple**, 7 = **yellow**, 8 = **black**, 9 = **pink**, 10 = **brown**

Numbers **0** to **3**

zero	one	two	three
0	**I**	**2**	**3**

Directions: Circle the correct number.

0   I   (2)   3

0   I   2   3

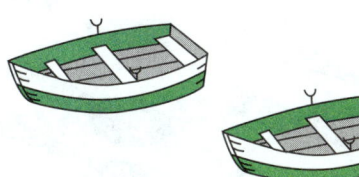

0   I   2   3

0   I   2   3

0   I   2   3

0   I   2   3

Math: Grade 1

Numbers 4 to 7

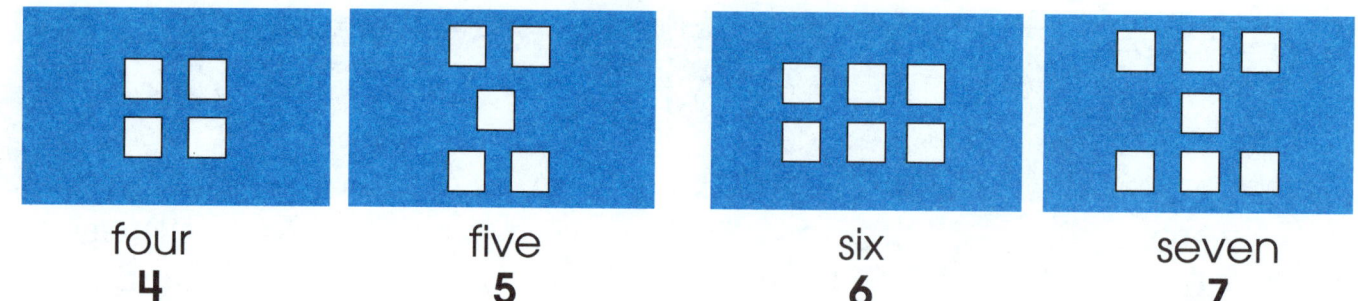

four
4

five
5

six
6

seven
7

Directions: Circle the correct number.

4   5   6   7

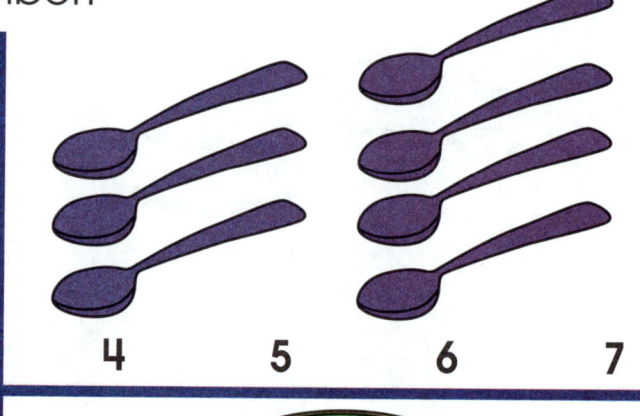

4   5   6   7

4   5   6   7

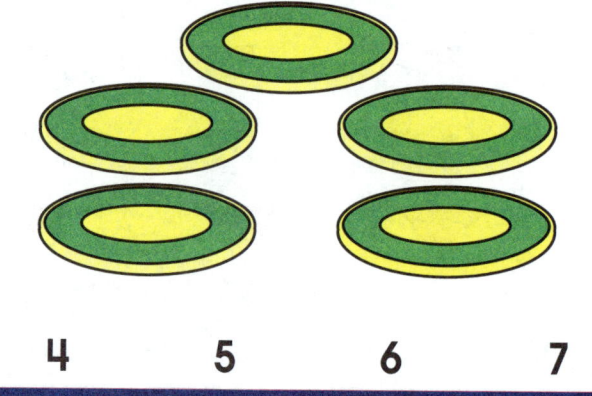

4   5   6   7

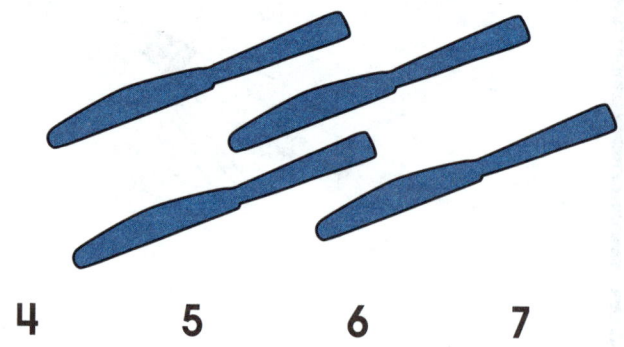

4   5   6   7

4   5   6   7

Subtracting

You and Oliver Opossum have **25¢** to buy some of these toys.

Directions: When you buy a toy, cross it out. Then, write the cost in the table. The first toy is crossed out for you. Each time you buy a toy, subtract it until you have **no more money** to spend.

25 ¢	–	**4** ¢	=	**21** ¢
21 ¢	–	_____ ¢	=	_____ ¢
_____ ¢	–	_____ ¢	=	_____ ¢
_____ ¢	–	_____ ¢	=	_____ ¢
_____ ¢	–	_____ ¢	=	_____ ¢
_____ ¢	–	_____ ¢	=	_____ ¢

Math: Grade 1

What's Left?

Directions: Look at the pictures. Complete the subtraction sentences.

6 - 2 = _____

9 - 5 = _____

7 - 2 = _____

4 - 1 = _____

8 - 1 = _____

4 - 0 = _____

Number Word Find

Directions: Find the number words **0** to **12** hidden in the box.

```
t  e  a  z  w  z  x  a  b  i  g  t  e  n
o  l  z  r  b  e  r  e  v  e  d  l  a  j
t  w  e  l  v  e  a  b  o  n  e  c  d  z
i  a  r  p  q  d  p  s  u  j  x  e  i  w
c  f  o  p  l  s  c  k  i  q  u  i  i  o
m  s  t  f  v  i  o  e  t  t  f  g  h  d
t  n  u  w  u  x  g  z  w  h  g  h  r  o
n  i  n  e  k  f  d  f  o  u  r  t  j  f
a  s  g  l  q  c  w  k  o  s  n  v  m  i
n  y  c  e  b  o  n  h  h  p  o  m  p  v
b  e  x  v  s  s  e  v  e  n  w  e  n  e
t  h  r  e  e  r  t  a  l  j  k  x  q  z
m  o  a  n  e  n  i  m  u  t  w  a  y  x
```

Words to find:

zero	four	eight	eleven
one	five	nine	twelve
two	six	ten	
three	seven		

11   *Math: Grade 1*

Ordinal Numbers

Directions: Ordinal numbers show the order in a series, such as first, second, or third. Follow the instructions to color the train cars. The first car is the engine.

Color the third car **blue**.

Color the eighth car **green**.

Color the fifth car **orange**.

Color the sixth car **yellow**.

Color the fourth car **brown**.

Color the second car **purple**.

Color the first car **red**.

Color the seventh car **pink**.

Ordinal Numbers

Directions: Write each word on the correct line to put the words in order.

| second | fifth | seventh | first | tenth |
| third | eighth | sixth | fourth | ninth |

1. _____   6. _____

2. _____   7. _____

3. _____   8. _____

4. _____   9. _____

5. _____   10. _____

Directions: Which picture is circled in each row? Underline the word that tells the correct number.

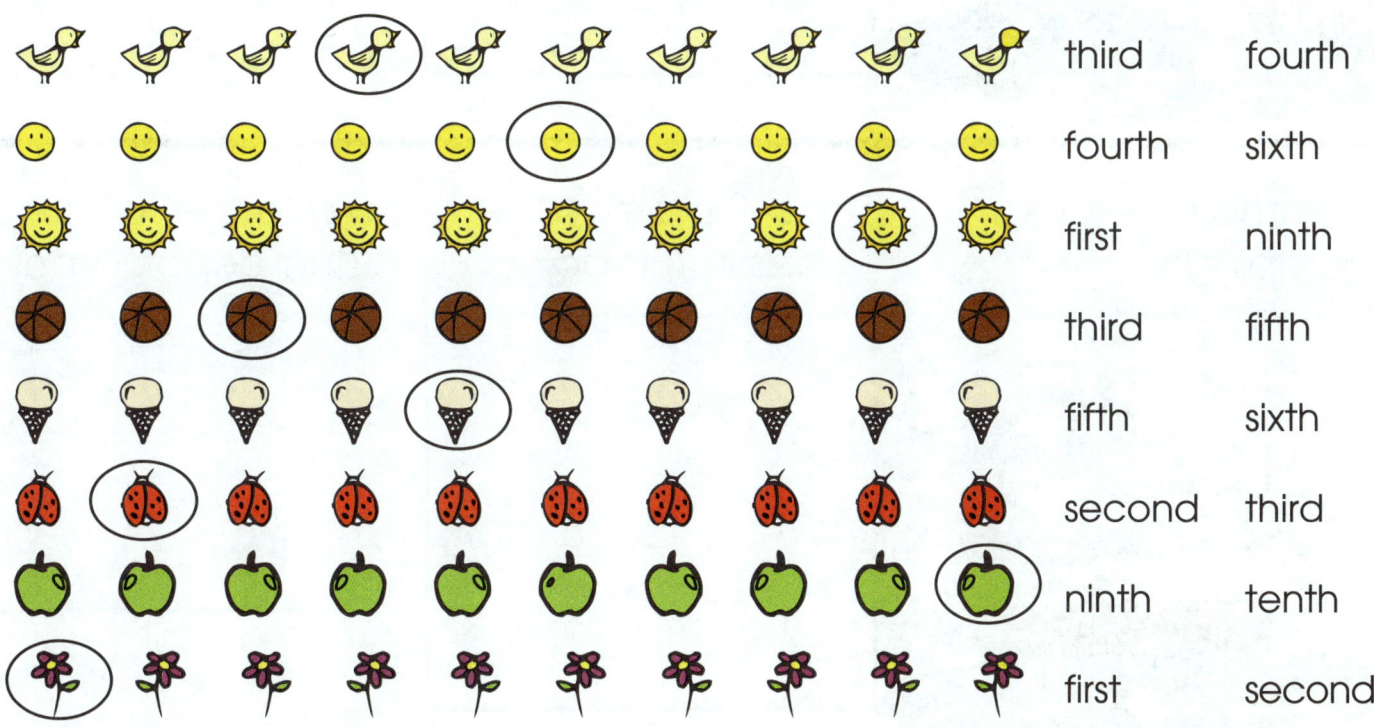

third	fourth
fourth	sixth
first	ninth
third	fifth
fifth	sixth
second	third
ninth	tenth
first	second

Addition

Putting numbers together is called **addition**. When you add two numbers together, you get a **total**, or **sum**. The symbol used for addition is called a **plus sign** (+). The symbol used for a total is an **equal sign** (=).

Directions: Follow the instructions below to create and solve the addition problems.

I pony is eating hay.	Draw I more pony in this box.	Write the total number of ponies.

I lamb is jumping.	Draw 2 more lambs in this box.	Write the total number of lambs.

I4

Addition

The geese are taking a stroll in the park.

Directions: Use crayons to color **2** geese **red**, **3** geese **green**, **4** geese **blue**, and **5** geese **yellow**.

Directions: Complete the addition equations to show how many geese of each color there are.

| green geese | $1 + \rule{1cm}{0.4pt} = 3$ | red geese | $\begin{array}{r} 1 \\ + \rule{1cm}{0.4pt} \\ \hline 2 \end{array}$ |
| blue geese | $2 + 2 = \rule{1cm}{0.4pt}$ | yellow geese | $\begin{array}{r} 1 \\ + \rule{1cm}{0.4pt} \\ \hline 5 \end{array}$ |

Math: Grade 1

Addition

Mrs. Murky asked 3 monster girls and 2 monster boys to come to the front of the class. She said, "If I have 3 monster girls and I add 2 monster boys, how many monster children do I have all together?"

Directions: Now, do the same problem on the board, but count the 2 boys first.

$$3 + 2 = \underline{\hspace{2em}}$$
$$2 + \underline{\hspace{2em}} = \underline{\hspace{2em}}$$

Does it matter which group is counted first? _____

Problem Solving

Directions: Solve each problem.

There are 5 white  .

There are 4 blue  .

How many in all?

There are 3  .

7 more  come.

How many are there now?

Beth has 9  .

She buys 1 more.

Now how many does she have?

There are 6 .

There are 3 .

How many in all?

There were 8  .

2 more came.

Then how many were there?

Math: Grade 1

Plenty to Wear!

Directions: The key words "in all" tell you to add. Circle the key words "in all" and solve the problems.

I. Jack has 4 white shirts and 2 yellow shirts. How many shirts does Jack have in all?

4 ◯ 2 = _____

2. Allison has 4 pink blouses and 6 red ones. How many blouses does Allison have in all?

4 ◯ 6 = _____

3. Betsy has 2 black skirts and 7 blue skirts. In all, how many skirts does Betsy have?

2 ◯ 7 = _____

4. Charley has 3 pairs of summer pants and 8 pairs of winter pants. How many pairs of pants does Charley have in all?

3 ◯ 8 = _____

5. Jeff has 5 knit hats and 5 cloth hats. How many hats does Jeff have in all?

5 ◯ 5 = _____

Calling All Cats

Directions: Look at the pictures. Complete the number sentences.

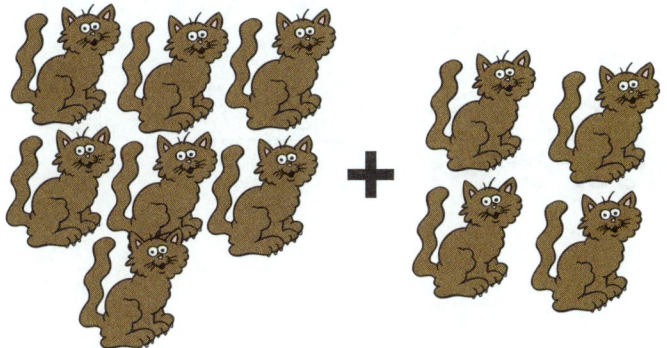

How many s are there in all?

7 ◯ 4 = _____

How many s are there in all?

6 ◯ 8 = _____

How many s are there in all?

11 ◯ 2 = _____

How many s are left?

13 ◯ 7 = _____

How many s are left?

9 ◯ 6 = _____

How many s are left?

12 ◯ 8 = _____

Math: Grade 1

Fractions: Halves $\frac{1}{2}$

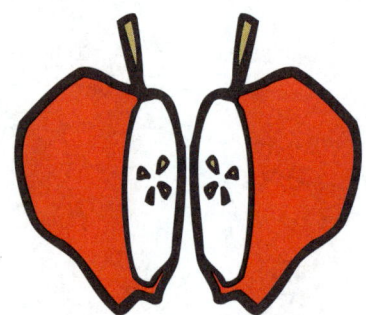

$\frac{1}{2}$ $\dfrac{\text{Part shaded or divided}}{\text{Number of equal parts}}$

Directions: Color only the shapes that show halves.

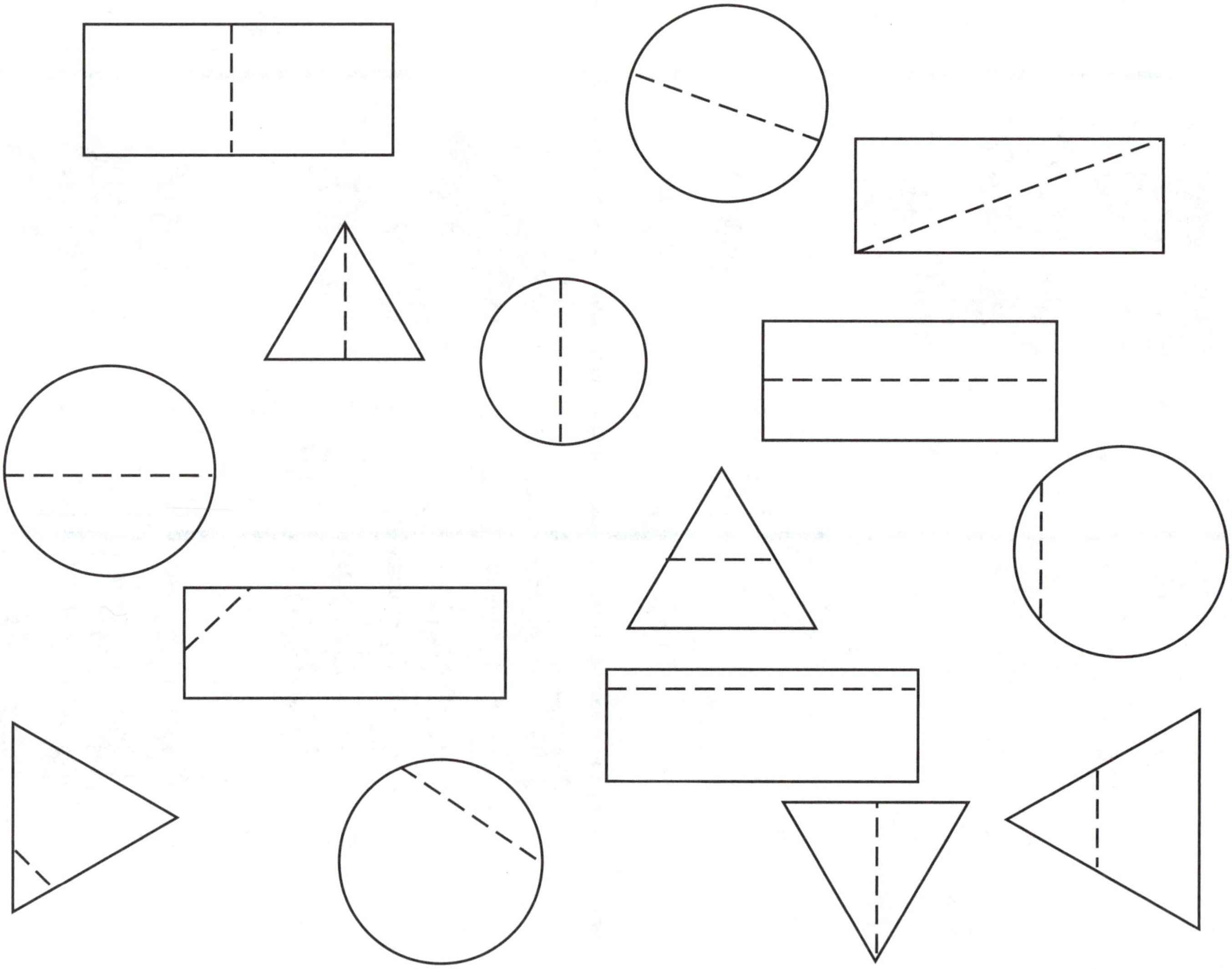

Fractions: Thirds $\frac{1}{3}$

Directions: Color the objects that have 3 equal parts.

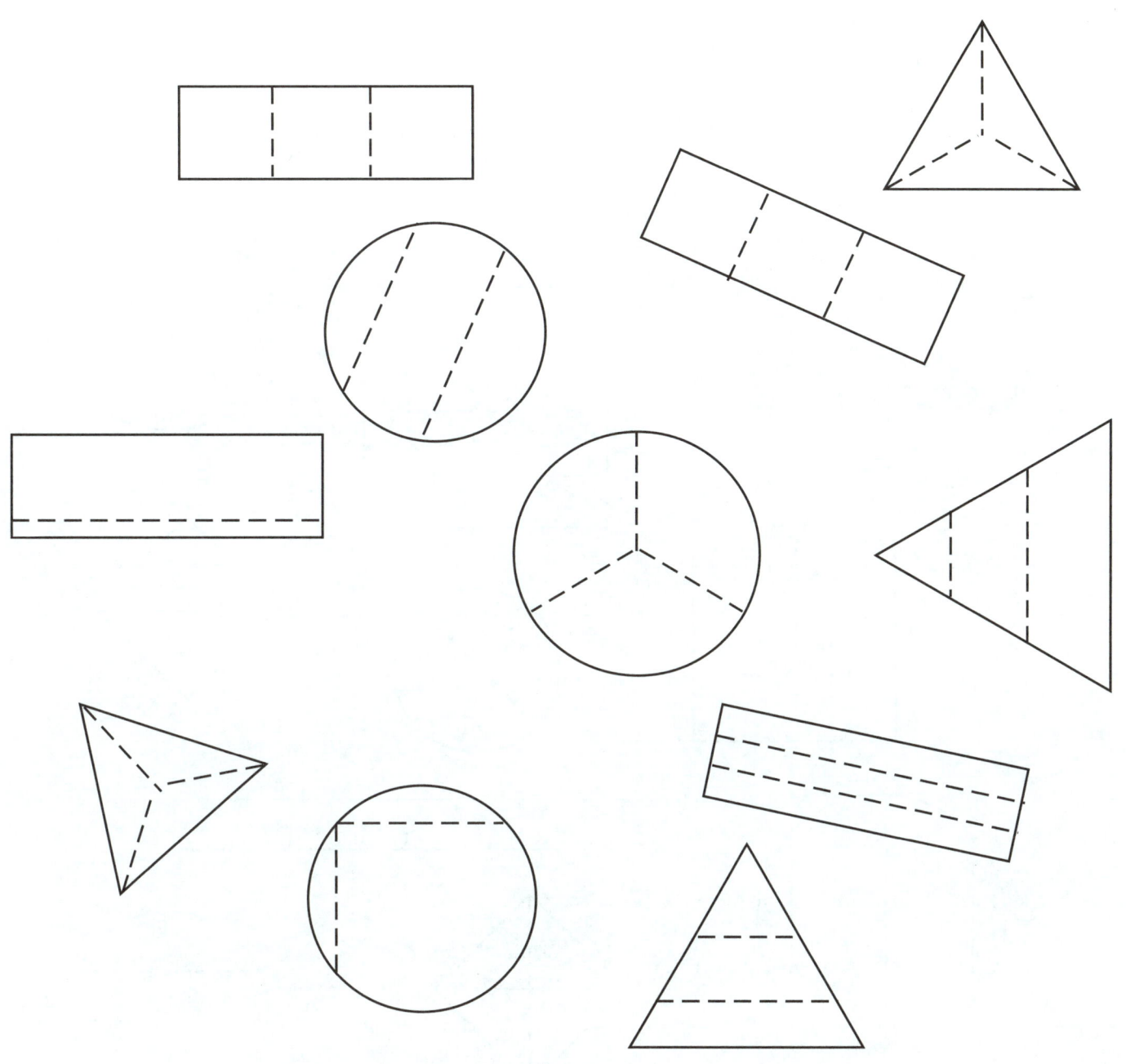

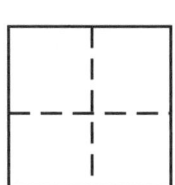

Fractions: Fourths $\frac{1}{4}$

Directions: Color the objects that have 4 equal parts.

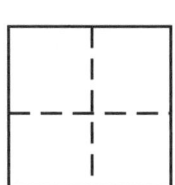
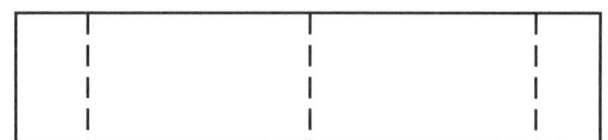
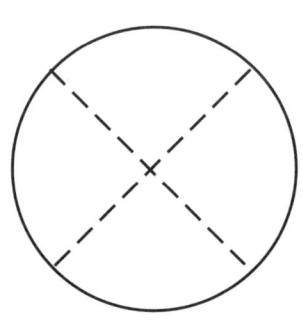
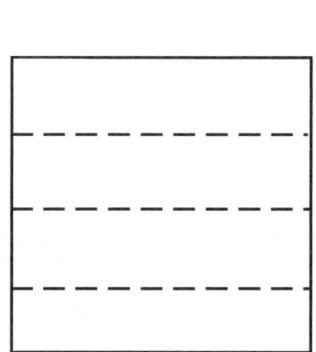
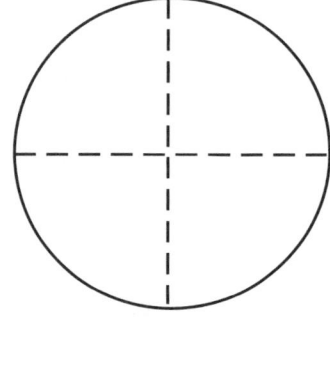
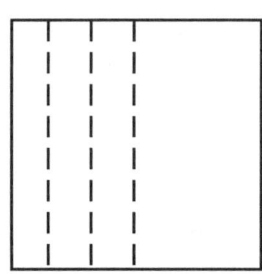
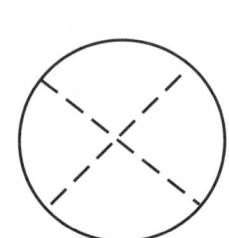
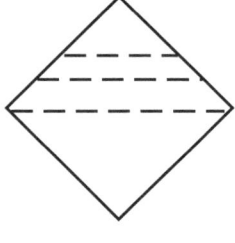
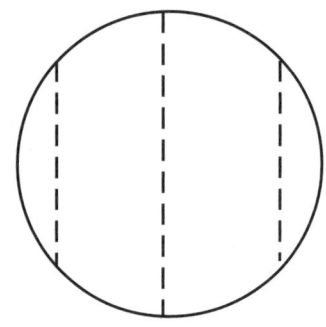
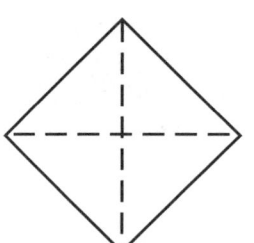
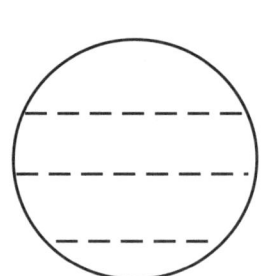

Fractions: Thirds and Fourths

Directions: Each object has 3 equal parts. Color one section.

Directions: Each object has 4 equal parts. Color one section.

 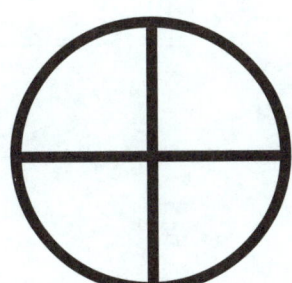 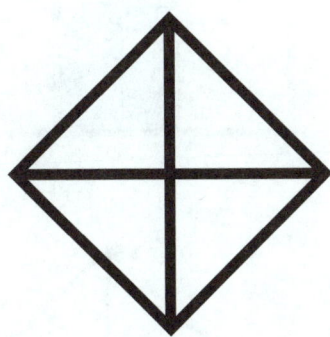

 Math: Grade 1

Review: Fractions

Directions: Count the equal parts. Then, write the fraction.

Example:

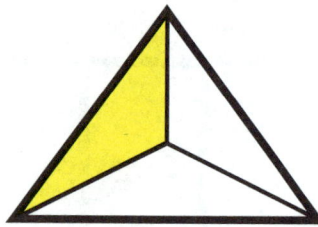

Shaded part = __1__

Equal parts = __3__

Write $\dfrac{1}{3}$

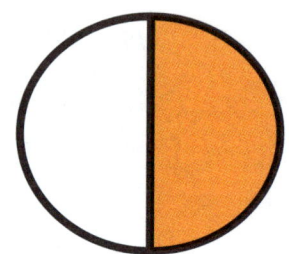

Shaded part = __1__

Equal parts = ____

Write ___

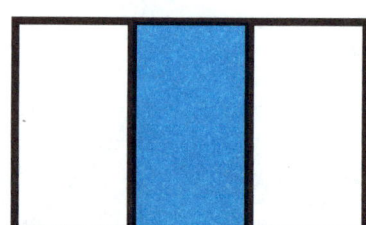

Shaded part = __1__

Equal parts = ____

Write ___

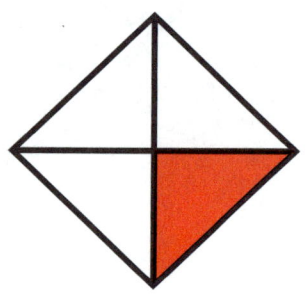

Shaded part = __1__

Equal parts = ____

Write ___

Fractions

The monsters are studying the moon. It changes its appearance as the month goes by. Sometimes the full moon is seen. Sometimes only part of it is seen. When only part of the moon is showing, it is a **fraction** of its full size.

Directions: Help the monsters learn fractions by filling in the blanks below.

Pretend the moon is divided into 2 equal parts.

$\dfrac{2}{2}$  The moon is full. The monsters see both of its 2 parts.

$\dfrac{1}{2}$  This is a half moon. The monsters see only _____ of its 2 parts.

What if you divided the moon into 4 equal parts?

$\dfrac{4}{4}$  The moon is full. The monsters can see all 4 of its _____ parts.

$\dfrac{3}{4}$  The moon is almost full. The monsters can see _____ of the 4 parts.

$\dfrac{}{4}$  The moon is half full. The monsters can see _____ of the 4 parts.

$\dfrac{}{4}$ The moon is almost gone. Only _____ part is left.

Math: Grade 1

Time: Hour

The short hand of the clock tells the hour. The long hand tells how many minutes after the hour. When the minute hand is on the **12**, it is the beginning of the hour.

Directions: Look at each clock. Write the time.

Example:

___**3**___ o'clock

_____ o'clock

_____ o'clock

_____ o'clock

_____ o'clock

_____ o'clock

_____ o'clock

_____ o'clock

_____ o'clock

Going Bananas!

Directions: Write an addition sentence for each problem.

Example:

2¢ + 5¢ = 7¢

_____

_____

_____

_____

_____

_____

_____

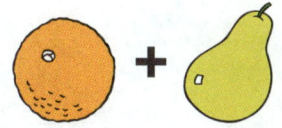

_____

_____

Math: Grade 1

Dimes

This is a dime.
It is worth **10** cents.

front

back

It has 2 sides. It has ridges on its edge.

Directions: Color the dimes silver or gray.

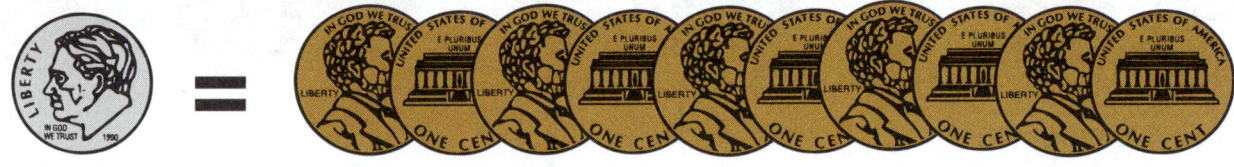

Directions: Write the amounts.

_____ dime = _____ pennies

_____ dime = _____ cents

_____ dime = _____ ¢

Counting With Dimes and Pennies

Directions: Count the dimes and the pennies.

Say ___10___ ___11___ ___12___ = ___12___ ¢
                                        Total

Begin with the dime, then add the pennies.

_____ _____ _____ _____ = _____ ¢

_____ _____ = _____ ¢

_____

_____ _____ _____ = _____ ¢

69

Penny, Nickel, Dime

A penny is worth one cent. It is written **1¢** or **$.01.** A nickel is worth five cents. It is written **5¢** or **$.05.** A dime is worth ten cents. It is written **10¢** or **$.10.**

Directions: Add the coins pictured and write the total amounts in the blanks.

Example:

dime **nickel** **nickel** **pennies**
10¢ = 5¢ + 5¢ = 10¢

10¢ + 1¢ = _____ ¢   10¢ + _____ ¢ = _____ ¢

_____ ¢ + _____ ¢ + _____ ¢ = _____ ¢

_____ ¢ + _____ ¢ = _____ ¢

Answer Key

Number Recognition 1, 2, 3, 4, 5

Directions: Use the color codes to color the parrot.
Color: 1 = red, 2 = blue, 3 = yellow, 4 = green, 5 = orange

3

Number Recognition 6, 7, 8, 9, 10

Directions: Use the color codes to color the carousel horse.
Color: 6 = purple, 7 = yellow, 8 = black, 9 = pink, 10 = brown

4

Numbers 0 to 3

zero 0 | one 1 | two 2 | three 3

Directions: Circle the correct number.

5

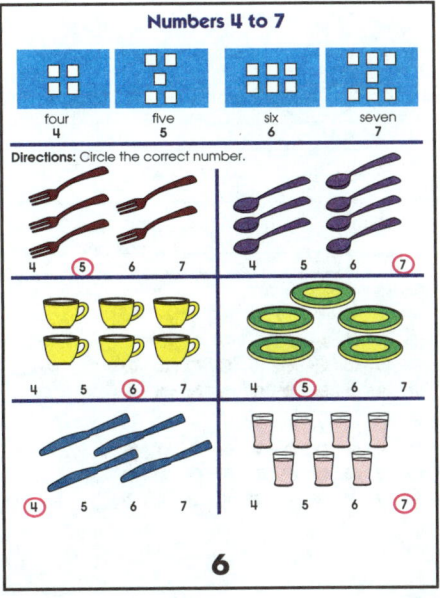

Numbers 4 to 7

four 4 | five 5 | six 6 | seven 7

Directions: Circle the correct number.

6

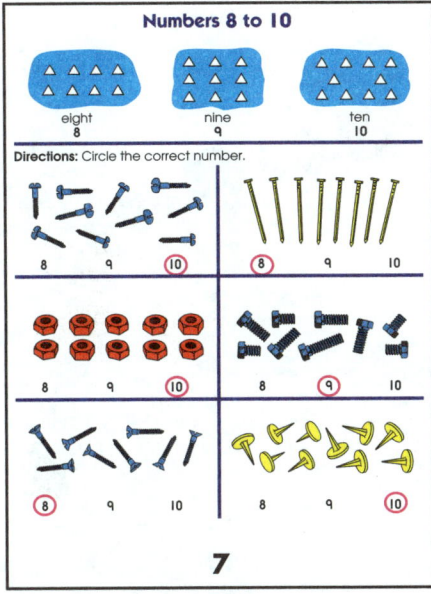

Numbers 8 to 10

eight 8 | nine 9 | ten 10

Directions: Circle the correct number.

7

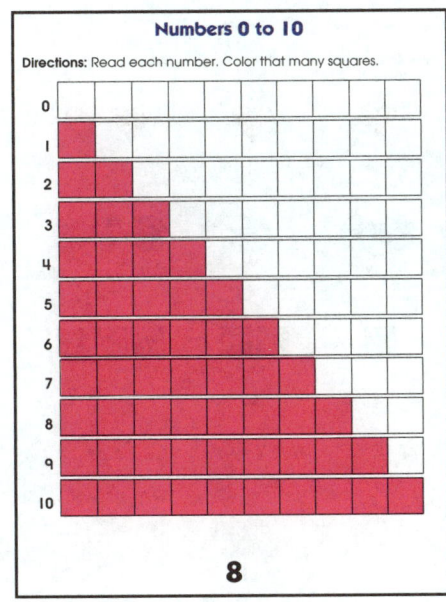

Numbers 0 to 10

Directions: Read each number. Color that many squares.

8

Number Words

Directions: Number the buildings from one to six.

Directions: Draw a line from the word to the number.

two — 1
five — 3
six — 5
four — 6
one — 2
three — 4

9

71 *Math: Grade 1*

Number Words

Directions: Number the buildings from five to ten.

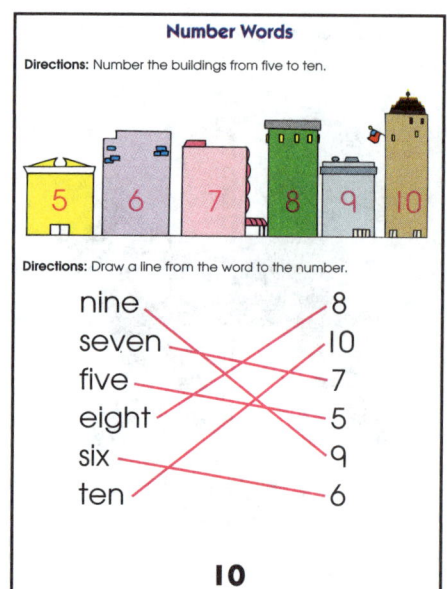

5 6 7 8 9 10

Directions: Draw a line from the word to the number.

nine — 8
seven — 10
five — 7
eight — 5
six — 9
ten — 6

10

Number Word Find

Directions: Find the number words **0** to **12** hidden in the box.

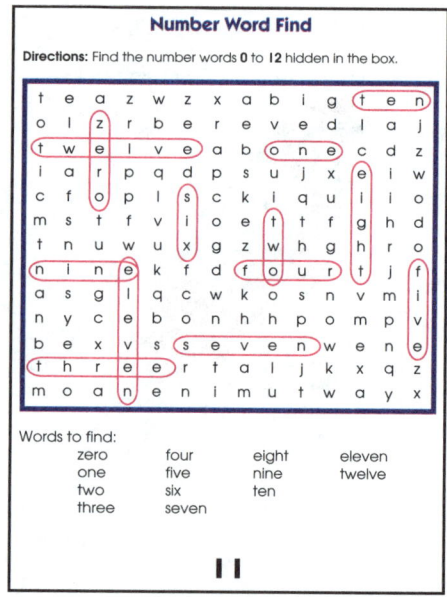

Words to find:

zero	four	eight	eleven
one	five	nine	twelve
two	six	ten	
three	seven		

11

Ordinal Numbers

Directions: Ordinal numbers show the order in a series, such as first, second, or third. Follow the instructions to color the train cars. The first car is the engine.

Color the third car **blue**.
Color the eighth car **green**.
Color the fifth car **orange**.
Color the sixth car **yellow**.
Color the fourth car **brown**.
Color the second car **purple**.
Color the first car **red**.
Color the seventh car **pink**.

12

Ordinal Numbers

Directions: Write each word on the correct line to put the words in order.

| second | fifth | seventh | first | tenth |
| third | eighth | sixth | fourth | ninth |

1. first   6. sixth
2. second   7. seventh
3. third   8. eighth
4. fourth   9. ninth
5. fifth   10. tenth

Directions: Which picture is circled in each row? Underline the word that tells the correct number.

third   **fourth**
fourth   **sixth**
first   **ninth**
third   fifth
fifth   sixth
second   third
ninth   **tenth**
first   second

13

Addition

Putting numbers together is called **addition**. When you add two numbers together, you get a **total**, or **sum**. The symbol used for addition is called a **plus sign** (+). The symbol used for a total is an **equal sign** (=).

Directions: Follow the instructions below to create and solve the addition problems.

1 pony is eating hay.   +   Draw 1 more pony in this box.   =   Write the total number of ponies.

2

1 lamb is jumping.   +   Draw 2 more lambs in this box.   =   Write the total number of lambs.

3

14

Addition 1, 2

Addition means "putting together" or adding two or more numbers to find the sum. "+" is a plus sign. It means to add the 2 numbers. "=" is an equals sign. It tells how much they are together.

Directions: Count the cats and tell how many.

2

3

4

15

Addition

Directions: Count the shapes and write the numbers below to tell how many in all.

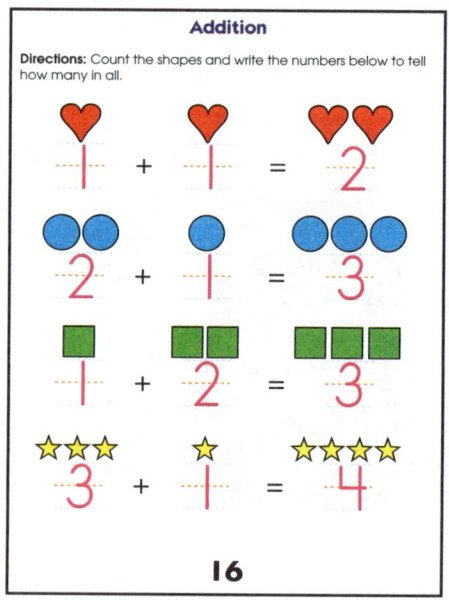

1 + 1 = 2

2 + 1 = 3

1 + 2 = 3

3 + 1 = 4

16

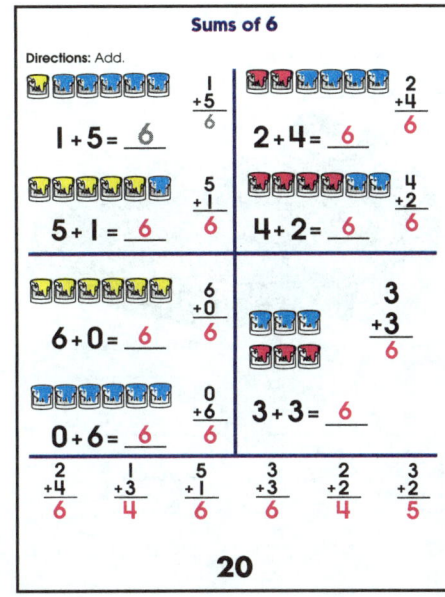

Addition

Directions: Draw the correct number of dots next to the numbers in each problem. Add up the number of dots to find your answer.

Example:

$$\begin{array}{r} 3 \\ + 2 \\ \hline 5 \end{array} \quad \cdots \qquad 2 + 2 = \underline{4}$$

$$\begin{array}{r} 4 \\ + 2 \\ \hline 6 \end{array} \qquad 1 + 5 = \underline{6}$$

$$\begin{array}{r} 3 \\ + 1 \\ \hline 4 \end{array} \qquad 4 + 3 = \underline{7}$$

$$\begin{array}{r} 6 \\ + 2 \\ \hline 8 \end{array} \qquad 5 + 3 = \underline{8}$$

17

Sums 0 to 3

Directions: Add.

$$\begin{array}{r} 1 \\ + 1 \\ \hline 2 \end{array}$$

$$1 + 1 = \underline{2}$$

$$2 + 1 = \underline{3} \qquad \begin{array}{r} 2 \\ + 1 \\ \hline 3 \end{array}$$

$$1 + 2 = \underline{3} \qquad \begin{array}{r} 1 \\ + 2 \\ \hline 3 \end{array}$$

$$2 + 0 = \underline{2} \qquad \begin{array}{r} 2 \\ + 0 \\ \hline 2 \end{array}$$

$$3 + 0 = \underline{3} \qquad \begin{array}{r} 3 \\ + 0 \\ \hline 3 \end{array}$$

$$0 + 2 = \underline{2} \qquad \begin{array}{r} 0 \\ + 2 \\ \hline 2 \end{array}$$

$$0 + 3 = \underline{3} \qquad \begin{array}{r} 0 \\ + 3 \\ \hline 3 \end{array}$$

$$\begin{array}{r} 0 \\ + 0 \\ \hline 0 \end{array}$$

$$0 + 0 = \underline{0}$$

$$1 + 0 = \underline{1} \qquad \begin{array}{r} 1 \\ + 0 \\ \hline 1 \end{array}$$

$$0 + 1 = \underline{1} \qquad \begin{array}{r} 0 \\ + 1 \\ \hline 1 \end{array}$$

18

Sums of 4 and 5

Directions: Add.

$$4 + 1 = \underline{5} \qquad \begin{array}{r} 4 \\ + 1 \\ \hline 5 \end{array} \qquad 2 + 3 = \underline{5} \qquad \begin{array}{r} 2 \\ + 3 \\ \hline 5 \end{array}$$

$$1 + 4 = \underline{5} \qquad \begin{array}{r} 1 \\ + 4 \\ \hline 5 \end{array} \qquad 3 + 2 = \underline{5} \qquad \begin{array}{r} 3 \\ + 2 \\ \hline 5 \end{array}$$

$$2 + 2 = \underline{4} \qquad \begin{array}{r} 2 \\ + 2 \\ \hline 4 \end{array} \qquad \begin{array}{r} 4 + 0 = \underline{4} \\ 0 + 4 = \underline{4} \end{array} \qquad \begin{array}{r} 4 \\ + 0 \\ \hline 4 \end{array} \quad \begin{array}{r} 0 \\ + 4 \\ \hline 4 \end{array}$$

$$5 + 0 = \underline{5} \qquad \begin{array}{r} 5 \\ + 0 \\ \hline 5 \end{array} \qquad 1 + 3 = \underline{4} \qquad \begin{array}{r} 1 \\ + 3 \\ \hline 4 \end{array}$$

$$0 + 5 = \underline{5} \qquad \begin{array}{r} 0 \\ + 5 \\ \hline 5 \end{array} \qquad 3 + 1 = \underline{4} \qquad \begin{array}{r} 3 \\ + 1 \\ \hline 4 \end{array}$$

19

Sums of 6

Directions: Add.

$$1 + 5 = \underline{6} \qquad \begin{array}{r} 1 \\ + 5 \\ \hline 6 \end{array} \qquad 2 + 4 = \underline{6} \qquad \begin{array}{r} 2 \\ + 4 \\ \hline 6 \end{array}$$

$$5 + 1 = \underline{6} \qquad \begin{array}{r} 5 \\ + 1 \\ \hline 6 \end{array} \qquad 4 + 2 = \underline{6} \qquad \begin{array}{r} 4 \\ + 2 \\ \hline 6 \end{array}$$

$$6 + 0 = \underline{6} \qquad \begin{array}{r} 6 \\ + 0 \\ \hline 6 \end{array} \qquad \begin{array}{r} 3 \\ + 3 \\ \hline 6 \end{array}$$

$$0 + 6 = \underline{6} \qquad \begin{array}{r} 0 \\ + 6 \\ \hline 6 \end{array} \qquad 3 + 3 = \underline{6}$$

$$\begin{array}{r} 2 \\ + 4 \\ \hline 6 \end{array} \quad \begin{array}{r} 1 \\ + 3 \\ \hline 4 \end{array} \quad \begin{array}{r} 5 \\ + 1 \\ \hline 6 \end{array} \quad \begin{array}{r} 3 \\ + 3 \\ \hline 6 \end{array} \quad \begin{array}{r} 2 \\ + 2 \\ \hline 4 \end{array} \quad \begin{array}{r} 3 \\ + 2 \\ \hline 5 \end{array}$$

20

Sums of 7

Directions: Add.

$$3 + 4 = \underline{7} \qquad \begin{array}{r} 3 \\ + 4 \\ \hline 7 \end{array} \qquad 6 + 1 = \underline{7} \qquad \begin{array}{r} 6 \\ + 1 \\ \hline 7 \end{array}$$

$$4 + 3 = \underline{7} \qquad \begin{array}{r} 4 \\ + 3 \\ \hline 7 \end{array} \qquad 1 + 6 = \underline{7} \qquad \begin{array}{r} 1 \\ + 6 \\ \hline 7 \end{array}$$

$$7 + 0 = \underline{7} \qquad \begin{array}{r} 7 \\ + 0 \\ \hline 7 \end{array} \qquad 2 + 5 = \underline{7} \qquad \begin{array}{r} 2 \\ + 5 \\ \hline 7 \end{array}$$

$$0 + 7 = \underline{7} \qquad \begin{array}{r} 0 \\ + 7 \\ \hline 7 \end{array} \qquad 5 + 2 = \underline{7} \qquad \begin{array}{r} 5 \\ + 2 \\ \hline 7 \end{array}$$

$$\begin{array}{r} 5 \\ + 2 \\ \hline 7 \end{array} \quad \begin{array}{r} 3 \\ + 3 \\ \hline 6 \end{array} \quad \begin{array}{r} 4 \\ + 3 \\ \hline 7 \end{array} \quad \begin{array}{r} 1 \\ + 6 \\ \hline 7 \end{array} \quad \begin{array}{r} 3 \\ + 4 \\ \hline 7 \end{array} \quad \begin{array}{r} 6 \\ + 0 \\ \hline 6 \end{array}$$

21

Sums of 8

Directions: Add.

$$5 + 3 = \underline{8} \qquad \begin{array}{r} 5 \\ + 3 \\ \hline 8 \end{array} \qquad 7 + 1 = \underline{8} \qquad \begin{array}{r} 7 \\ + 1 \\ \hline 8 \end{array}$$

$$3 + 5 = \underline{8} \qquad \begin{array}{r} 3 \\ + 5 \\ \hline 8 \end{array} \qquad 1 + 7 = \underline{8} \qquad \begin{array}{r} 1 \\ + 7 \\ \hline 8 \end{array}$$

$$2 + 6 = \underline{8} \qquad \begin{array}{r} 2 \\ + 6 \\ \hline 8 \end{array} \qquad \begin{array}{r} 4 \\ + 4 \\ \hline 8 \end{array}$$

$$6 + 2 = \underline{8} \qquad \begin{array}{r} 6 \\ + 2 \\ \hline 8 \end{array} \qquad 4 + 4 = \underline{8}$$

$$\begin{array}{r} 3 \\ + 3 \\ \hline 6 \end{array} \quad \begin{array}{r} 5 \\ + 3 \\ \hline 8 \end{array} \quad \begin{array}{r} 2 \\ + 6 \\ \hline 8 \end{array} \quad \begin{array}{r} 8 \\ + 0 \\ \hline 8 \end{array} \quad \begin{array}{r} 4 \\ + 3 \\ \hline 7 \end{array} \quad \begin{array}{r} 0 \\ + 8 \\ \hline 8 \end{array}$$

22

Sums of 9

Directions: Add.

$$2 + 7 = \underline{9} \qquad \begin{array}{r} 2 \\ + 7 \\ \hline 9 \end{array} \qquad 5 + 4 = \underline{9} \qquad \begin{array}{r} 5 \\ + 4 \\ \hline 9 \end{array}$$

$$7 + 2 = \underline{9} \qquad \begin{array}{r} 7 \\ + 2 \\ \hline 9 \end{array} \qquad 4 + 5 = \underline{9} \qquad \begin{array}{r} 4 \\ + 5 \\ \hline 9 \end{array}$$

$$1 + 8 = \underline{9} \qquad \begin{array}{r} 1 \\ + 8 \\ \hline 9 \end{array} \qquad 3 + 6 = \underline{9} \qquad \begin{array}{r} 3 \\ + 6 \\ \hline 9 \end{array}$$

$$8 + 1 = \underline{9} \qquad \begin{array}{r} 8 \\ + 1 \\ \hline 9 \end{array} \qquad 6 + 3 = \underline{9} \qquad \begin{array}{r} 6 \\ + 3 \\ \hline 9 \end{array}$$

$$0 + 9 = \underline{9} \qquad \begin{array}{r} 0 \\ + 9 \\ \hline 9 \end{array} \qquad 9 + 0 = \underline{9} \qquad \begin{array}{r} 9 \\ + 0 \\ \hline 9 \end{array}$$

$$\begin{array}{r} 5 \\ + 4 \\ \hline 9 \end{array} \quad \begin{array}{r} 3 \\ + 6 \\ \hline 9 \end{array} \quad \begin{array}{r} 8 \\ + 1 \\ \hline 9 \end{array} \quad \begin{array}{r} 4 \\ + 5 \\ \hline 9 \end{array} \quad \begin{array}{r} 7 \\ + 2 \\ \hline 9 \end{array} \quad \begin{array}{r} 0 \\ + 8 \\ \hline 8 \end{array}$$

23

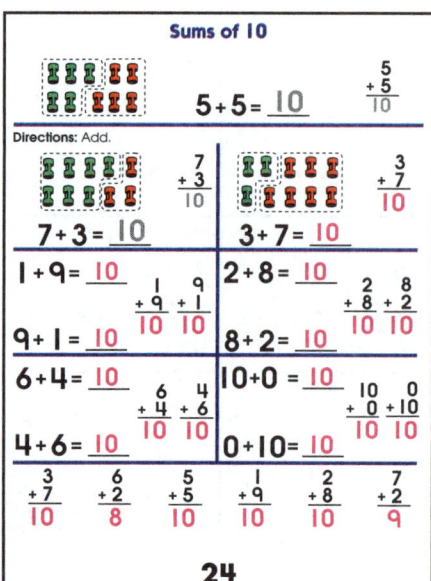

Sums of 10

$5 + 5 = \underline{10}$

$\begin{array}{r} 5 \\ + 5 \\ \hline 10 \end{array}$

Directions: Add.

$\begin{array}{r} 7 \\ + 3 \\ \hline 10 \end{array}$ $\begin{array}{r} 3 \\ + 7 \\ \hline 10 \end{array}$

$7 + 3 = \underline{10}$ $3 + 7 = \underline{10}$

$1 + 9 = \underline{10}$ $\begin{array}{r} 1 \\ + 9 \\ \hline 10 \end{array}$ $\begin{array}{r} 9 \\ + 1 \\ \hline 10 \end{array}$ $2 + 8 = \underline{10}$ $\begin{array}{r} 2 \\ + 8 \\ \hline 10 \end{array}$ $\begin{array}{r} 8 \\ + 2 \\ \hline 10 \end{array}$

$9 + 1 = \underline{10}$ $8 + 2 = \underline{10}$

$6 + 4 = \underline{10}$ $\begin{array}{r} 6 \\ + 4 \\ \hline 10 \end{array}$ $\begin{array}{r} 4 \\ + 6 \\ \hline 10 \end{array}$ $10 + 0 = \underline{10}$ $\begin{array}{r} 10 \\ + 0 \\ \hline 10 \end{array}$ $\begin{array}{r} 0 \\ + 10 \\ \hline 10 \end{array}$

$4 + 6 = \underline{10}$ $0 + 10 = \underline{10}$

$\begin{array}{r} 3 \\ + 7 \\ \hline 10 \end{array}$ $\begin{array}{r} 6 \\ + 2 \\ \hline 8 \end{array}$ $\begin{array}{r} 5 \\ + 5 \\ \hline 10 \end{array}$ $\begin{array}{r} 1 \\ + 9 \\ \hline 10 \end{array}$ $\begin{array}{r} 2 \\ + 8 \\ \hline 10 \end{array}$ $\begin{array}{r} 7 \\ + 2 \\ \hline 9 \end{array}$

24

Addition

The Barton family is having a picnic. But the ants have carried away their food.

Directions: Use an addition equation to find out how many ants took food. The first one is done for you.

How many ants carried away fruit? $\underline{1} + \underline{2} = \underline{3}$

How many ants carried away vegetables? $\underline{2} + \underline{3} = \underline{5}$

How many ants carried away hot dogs? $\underline{3} + \underline{3} = \underline{6}$

How many ants carried away bread? $\underline{5} + \underline{2} = \underline{7}$

25

Addition

Directions: Add up the dots on the domino pieces below. Write the total on the line below each piece.

$+$ $+$ $+$

$\underline{8}$ $\underline{10}$ $\underline{6}$

Directions: Now, draw the missing dots on each domino. Make sure the total number of dots adds up to the total on the line below each domino.

$+$ $+$ $+$

$\underline{7}$ $\underline{9}$ $\underline{5}$

26

Addition

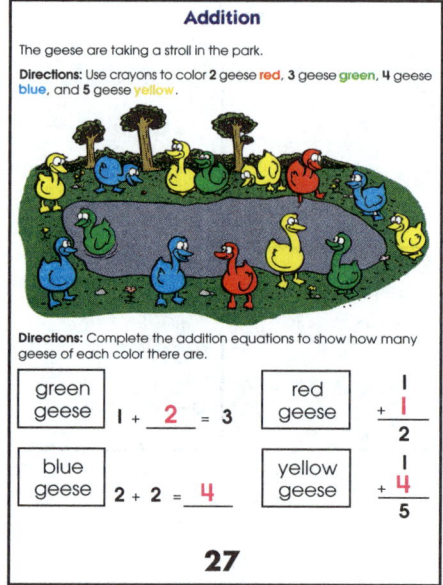

The geese are taking a stroll in the park.

Directions: Use crayons to color **2** geese **red**, **3** geese **green**, **4** geese **blue**, and **5** geese **yellow**.

Directions: Complete the addition equations to show how many geese of each color there are.

| green geese | $1 + \underline{2} = 3$ | red geese | $\begin{array}{r} 1 \\ + 1 \\ \hline 2 \end{array}$ |
| blue geese | $2 + 2 = \underline{4}$ | yellow geese | $\begin{array}{r} 1 \\ + 4 \\ \hline 5 \end{array}$ |

27

Addition

Mrs. Murky asked 3 monster girls and 2 monster boys to come to the front of the class. She said, "If I have 3 monster girls and I add 2 monster boys, how many monster children do I have all together?"

Directions: Now, do the same problem on the board, but count the 2 boys first.

$3 + 2 = \underline{5}$
$2 + \underline{3} = \underline{5}$

Does it matter which group is counted first? ___no___

28

Problem Solving

Directions: Solve each problem.

There are 5 white 🦋.
There are 4 blue 🦋.
How many in all?

$\begin{array}{r} 5 \\ + 4 \\ \hline 9 \end{array}$

There are 3 🐑.
7 more 🐑 come.
How many are there now?

$\begin{array}{r} 3 \\ + 7 \\ \hline 10 \end{array}$

Beth has 9 🧢.
She buys 1 more.
Now how many does she have?

$\begin{array}{r} 9 \\ + 1 \\ \hline 10 \end{array}$

There are 6 🕯.
There are 3 🕯.
How many in all?

$\begin{array}{r} 6 \\ + 3 \\ \hline 9 \end{array}$

There were 8 🐕.
2 more came.
Then how many were there?

$\begin{array}{r} 8 \\ + 2 \\ \hline 10 \end{array}$

29

Plenty to Wear!

Directions: The key words "in all" tell you to add. Circle the key words "in all" and solve the problems.

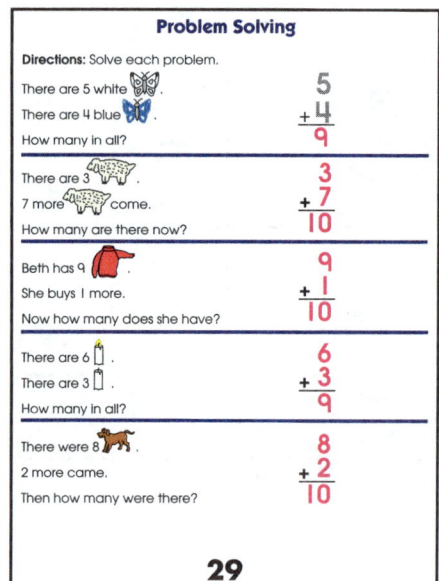

1. Jack has 4 white shirts and 2 yellow shirts. How many shirts does Jack have (in all)?

$4 \oplus 2 = \underline{6}$

2. Allison has 4 pink blouses and 6 red ones. How many blouses does Allison have (in all)?

$4 \oplus 6 = \underline{10}$

3. Betsy has 2 black skirts and 7 blue skirts (in all), how many skirts does Betsy have?

$2 \oplus 7 = \underline{9}$

4. Charley has 3 pairs of summer pants and 8 pairs of winter pants. How many pairs of pants does Charley have (in all)?

$3 \oplus 8 = \underline{11}$

5. Jeff has 5 knit hats and 5 cloth hats. How many hats does Jeff have (in all)?

$5 \oplus 5 = \underline{10}$

30

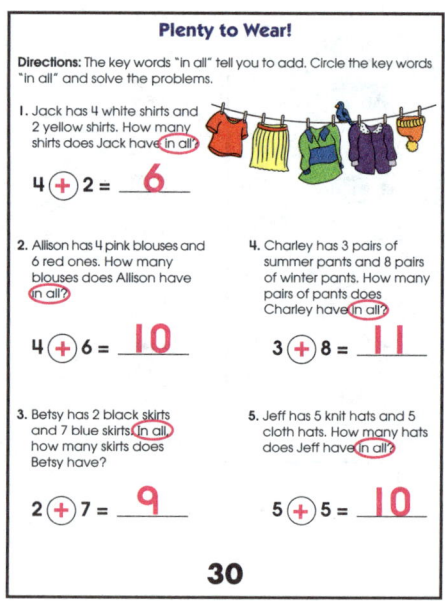

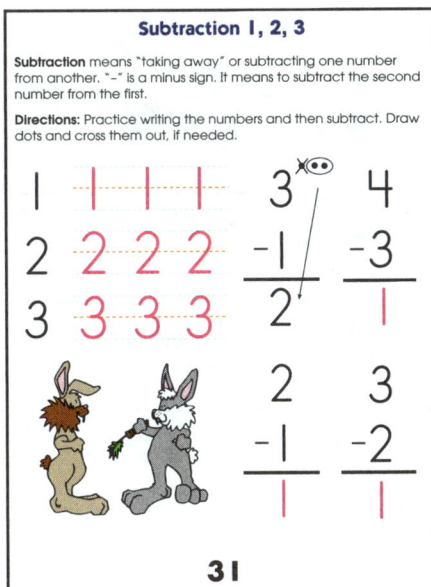

Subtraction 1, 2, 3

Subtraction means "taking away" or subtracting one number from another. "–" is a minus sign. It means to subtract the second number from the first.

Directions: Practice writing the numbers and then subtract. Draw dots and cross them out, if needed.

1 | | |

2 2 2 2

3 3 3 3

$$3 \atop -1 \over 2$$ $$4 \atop -3 \over 1$$

$$2 \atop -1 \over 1$$ $$3 \atop -2 \over 1$$

31

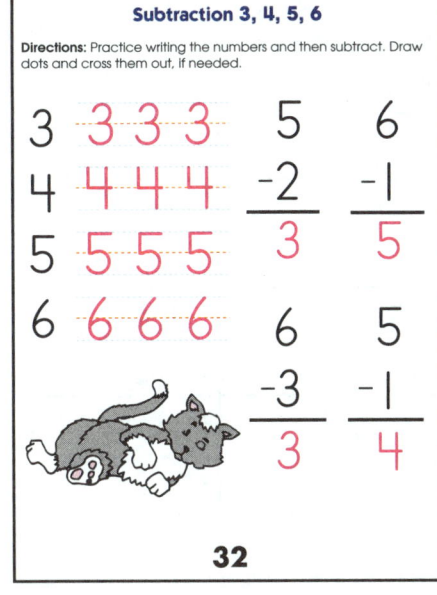

Subtraction 3, 4, 5, 6

Directions: Practice writing the numbers and then subtract. Draw dots and cross them out, if needed.

3 3 3 3

4 4 4 4

5 5 5 5

6 6 6 6

$$5 \atop -2 \over 3$$ $$6 \atop -1 \over 5$$

$$6 \atop -3 \over 3$$ $$5 \atop -1 \over 4$$

32

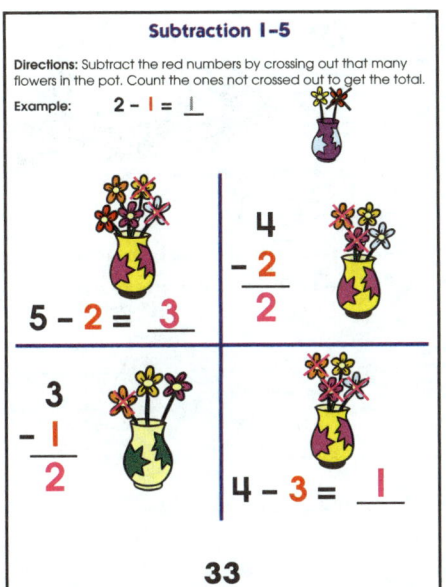

Subtraction 1–5

Directions: Subtract the red numbers by crossing out that many flowers in the pot. Count the ones not crossed out to get the total.

Example: 2 – 1 = 1

5 – 2 = 3

$$4 \atop -2 \over 2$$

$$3 \atop -1 \over 2$$

4 – 3 = 1

33

Subtraction 6–10

Directions: Count the flowers. Write your answer on the blank. Circle the problem that matches your answer.

9

$$10 \atop -1$$ $$9 \atop -1$$

6

$$7 \atop -2$$ $$9 \atop -3$$

8

$$9 \atop -6$$ $$8 \atop -0$$

7

$$10 \atop -2$$ $$8 \atop -1$$

34

Subtracting From 1, 2, and 3

Directions: Subtract.

$$3 \atop -1 \over 2$$

3 – 1 = 2

$$2 \atop -1 \over 1$$

2 – 1 = 1

$$3 \atop -2 \over 1$$

3 – 2 = 1

$$1 \atop -0 \over 1$$

1 – 0 = 1

$$3 \atop -0 \over 3$$

3 – 0 = 3

$$1 \atop -1 \over 0$$

1 – 1 = 0

$$2 \atop -2 \over 0$$

2 – 2 = 0

$$3 \atop -3 \over 0$$

3 – 3 = 0

35

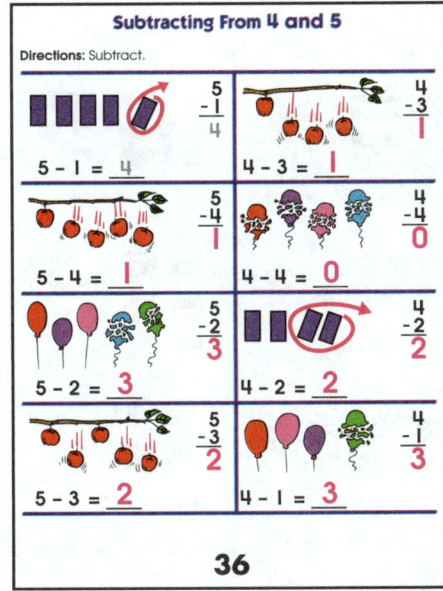

Subtracting From 4 and 5

Directions: Subtract.

$$5 \atop -1 \over 4$$

5 – 1 = 4

$$4 \atop -3 \over 1$$

4 – 3 = 1

$$5 \atop -4 \over 1$$

5 – 4 = 1

$$4 \atop -4 \over 0$$

4 – 4 = 0

$$5 \atop -2 \over 3$$

5 – 2 = 3

$$4 \atop -2 \over 2$$

4 – 2 = 2

$$5 \atop -3 \over 2$$

5 – 3 = 2

$$4 \atop -1 \over 3$$

4 – 1 = 3

36

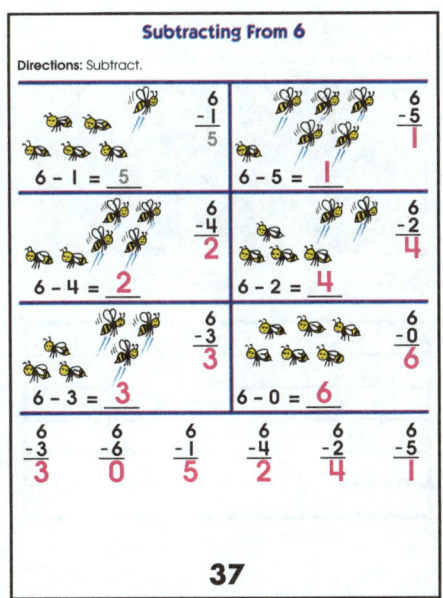

Subtracting From 6

Directions: Subtract.

$$6 \atop -1 \over 5$$

6 – 1 = 5

$$6 \atop -5 \over 1$$

6 – 5 = 1

$$6 \atop -4 \over 2$$

6 – 4 = 2

$$6 \atop -2 \over 4$$

6 – 2 = 4

$$6 \atop -3 \over 3$$

6 – 3 = 3

$$6 \atop -0 \over 6$$

6 – 0 = 6

$$6 \atop -3 \over 3$$ $$6 \atop -6 \over 0$$ $$6 \atop -1 \over 5$$ $$6 \atop -4 \over 2$$ $$6 \atop -2 \over 4$$ $$6 \atop -5 \over 1$$

37

75 *Math: Grade 1*

Subtracting From 7

Directions: Subtract.

$$\begin{array}{r} 7 \\ -6 \\ \hline 1 \end{array}$$

7 − 6 = 1

$$\begin{array}{r} 7 \\ -1 \\ \hline 6 \end{array}$$

7 − 1 = 6

$$\begin{array}{r} 7 \\ -3 \\ \hline 4 \end{array}$$

7 − 3 = 4

$$\begin{array}{r} 7 \\ -4 \\ \hline 3 \end{array}$$

7 − 4 = 3

$$\begin{array}{r} 7 \\ -7 \\ \hline 0 \end{array}$$

7 − 7 = 0

$$\begin{array}{r} 7 \\ -0 \\ \hline 7 \end{array}$$

7 − 0 = 7

$$\begin{array}{r} 7 \\ -2 \\ \hline 5 \end{array}$$

7 − 2 = 5

$$\begin{array}{r} 7 \\ -5 \\ \hline 2 \end{array}$$

7 − 5 = 2

38

Subtracting From 8

Directions: Subtract.

$$\begin{array}{r} 8 \\ -7 \\ \hline 1 \end{array}$$

8 − 7 = 1

$$\begin{array}{r} 8 \\ -1 \\ \hline 7 \end{array}$$

8 − 1 = 7

$$\begin{array}{r} 8 \\ -2 \\ \hline 6 \end{array}$$

8 − 2 = 6

$$\begin{array}{r} 8 \\ -6 \\ \hline 2 \end{array}$$

8 − 6 = 2

$$\begin{array}{r} 8 \\ -4 \\ \hline 4 \end{array}$$

8 − 4 = 4

$$\begin{array}{r} 8 \\ -8 \\ \hline 0 \end{array}$$

8 − 8 = 0

$$\begin{array}{r} 8 \\ -3 \\ \hline 5 \end{array}$$

8 − 3 = 5

$$\begin{array}{r} 8 \\ -5 \\ \hline 3 \end{array}$$

8 − 5 = 3

39

Subtracting From 9

Directions: Subtract.

$$\begin{array}{r} 9 \\ -6 \\ \hline 3 \end{array}$$

9 − 6 = 3

$$\begin{array}{r} 9 \\ -3 \\ \hline 6 \end{array}$$

9 − 3 = 6

$$\begin{array}{r} 9 \\ -0 \\ \hline 9 \end{array}$$

9 − 0 = 9

$$\begin{array}{r} 9 \\ -9 \\ \hline 0 \end{array}$$

9 − 9 = 0

$$\begin{array}{r} 9 \\ -5 \\ \hline 4 \end{array}$$

9 − 5 = 4

$$\begin{array}{r} 9 \\ -4 \\ \hline 5 \end{array}$$

9 − 4 = 5

$$\begin{array}{r} 9 \\ -8 \\ \hline 1 \end{array}$$

9 − 8 = 1

$$\begin{array}{r} 9 \\ -1 \\ \hline 8 \end{array}$$

9 − 1 = 8

$$\begin{array}{r} 9 \\ -2 \\ \hline 7 \end{array}$$

9 − 2 = 7

$$\begin{array}{r} 9 \\ -7 \\ \hline 2 \end{array}$$

9 − 7 = 2

40

Subtracting From 10

$$\begin{array}{r} 10 \\ -5 \\ \hline 5 \end{array}$$

10 − 5 = 5

$$\begin{array}{r} 10 \\ -10 \\ \hline 0 \end{array}$$

10 − 10 = 0

Directions: Subtract.

$$\begin{array}{r} 10 \\ -1 \\ \hline 9 \end{array}$$

10 − 1 = 9

$$\begin{array}{r} 10 \\ -9 \\ \hline 1 \end{array}$$

10 − 9 = 1

10 − 7 = 3

$$\begin{array}{r} 10 \\ -7 \\ \hline 3 \end{array}\quad\begin{array}{r} 10 \\ -3 \\ \hline 7 \end{array}$$

10 − 4 = 6

$$\begin{array}{r} 10 \\ -4 \\ \hline 6 \end{array}\quad\begin{array}{r} 10 \\ -6 \\ \hline 4 \end{array}$$

10 − 3 = 7

10 − 6 = 4

10 − 8 = 2

$$\begin{array}{r} 10 \\ -8 \\ \hline 2 \end{array}\quad\begin{array}{r} 10 \\ -2 \\ \hline 8 \end{array}$$

10 − 0 = 10

$$\begin{array}{r} 10 \\ -0 \\ \hline 10 \end{array}$$

10 − 2 = 8

$$\begin{array}{r} 10 \\ -7 \\ \hline 3 \end{array}\quad\begin{array}{r} 10 \\ -1 \\ \hline 9 \end{array}\quad\begin{array}{r} 10 \\ -5 \\ \hline 5 \end{array}\quad\begin{array}{r} 10 \\ -10 \\ \hline 0 \end{array}\quad\begin{array}{r} 10 \\ -2 \\ \hline 8 \end{array}\quad\begin{array}{r} 10 \\ -6 \\ \hline 4 \end{array}$$

41

How Many Animals Are Left?

Directions: The key word **left** tells you to subtract. Circle the key word **left**. Write a number sentence to solve each subtraction problem.

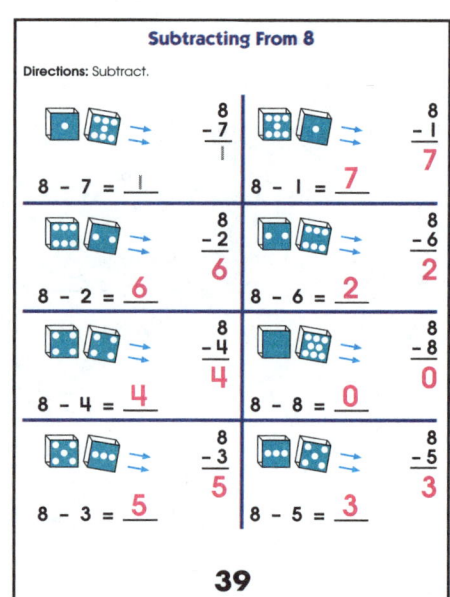

1. Bill had 10 kittens, but 4 of them ran away. How many kittens does he have left?

   10 − 4 = 6

2. There were 12 rabbits eating in the garden. Dogs chased 3 of them away. How many rabbits were left?

   12 − 3 = 9

3. There were 14 frogs on the bank of the pond. Then, 9 of them hopped into the water. How many frogs were left on the bank?

   14 − 9 = 5

4. Bill saw 11 birds eating from the bird feeders in his backyard. A cat scared 7 of them away. How many birds were left at the feeders?

   11 − 7 = 4

5. Bill counted 15 robins in his yard. Then, 8 of the robins flew away. How many robins were left in the yard?

   15 − 8 = 7

42

Subtracting

You and Oliver Opossum have **25¢** to buy some of these toys.

Directions: When you buy a toy, cross it out. Then, write the cost in the table. The first toy is crossed out for you. Each time you buy a toy, subtract it until you have **no more money** to spend.

25 ¢ −	4 ¢ =	21 ¢
21 ¢ −	¢ =	¢
¢ −	¢ =	¢
¢ −	¢ =	¢
¢ −	¢ =	¢
¢ −	¢ =	¢

Answers will vary.

43

What's Left?

Directions: Look at the pictures. Complete the subtraction sentences.

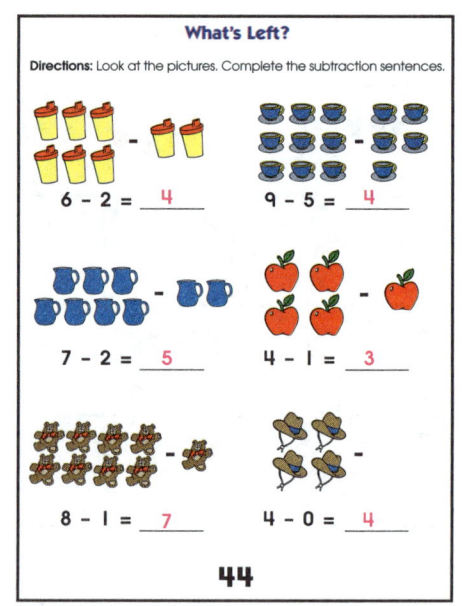

6 − 2 = 4

9 − 5 = 4

7 − 2 = 5

4 − 1 = 3

8 − 1 = 7

4 − 0 = 4

44

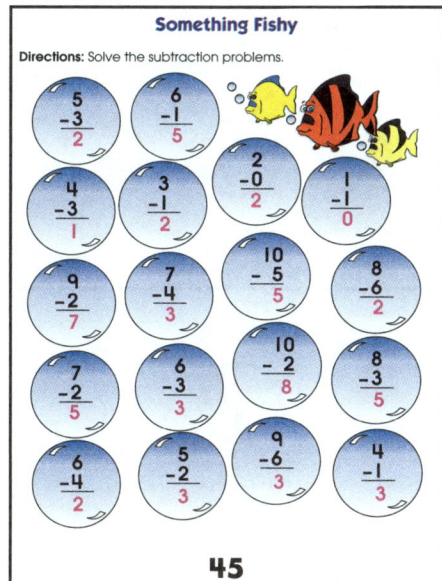

Something Fishy

Directions: Solve the subtraction problems.

$$5 - 3 = 2$$
$$6 - 1 = 5$$
$$2 - 0 = 2$$
$$1 - 1 = 0$$
$$4 - 3 = 1$$
$$3 - 1 = 2$$
$$9 - 2 = 7$$
$$7 - 4 = 3$$
$$10 - 5 = 5$$
$$8 - 6 = 2$$
$$7 - 2 = 5$$
$$6 - 3 = 3$$
$$10 - 2 = 8$$
$$8 - 3 = 5$$
$$6 - 4 = 2$$
$$5 - 2 = 3$$
$$9 - 6 = 3$$
$$4 - 1 = 3$$

45

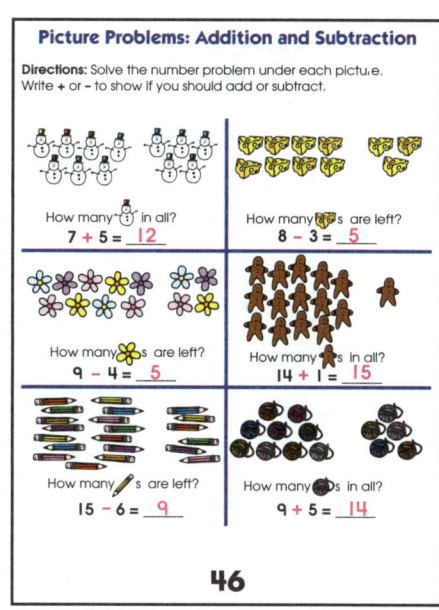

Picture Problems: Addition and Subtraction

Directions: Solve the number problem under each picture. Write + or – to show if you should add or subtract.

How many ☃s in all?
$$7 + 5 = 12$$

How many 🐯s are left?
$$8 - 3 = 5$$

How many 🌼s are left?
$$9 - 4 = 5$$

How many 🍪s in all?
$$14 + 1 = 15$$

How many ✏️s are left?
$$15 - 6 = 9$$

How many ☕s in all?
$$9 + 5 = 14$$

46

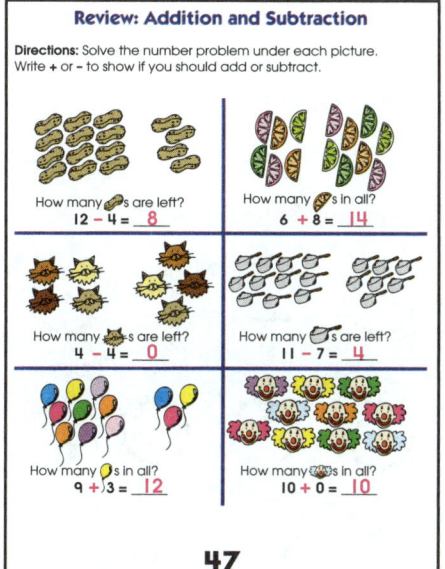

Review: Addition and Subtraction

Directions: Solve the number problem under each picture. Write + or – to show if you should add or subtract.

How many 🥜s are left?
$$12 - 4 = 8$$

How many 🍊s in all?
$$6 + 8 = 14$$

How many 🐱s are left?
$$4 - 4 = 0$$

How many 🦋s are left?
$$11 - 7 = 4$$

How many 🎈s in all?
$$9 + 3 = 12$$

How many 🤡s in all?
$$10 + 0 = 10$$

47

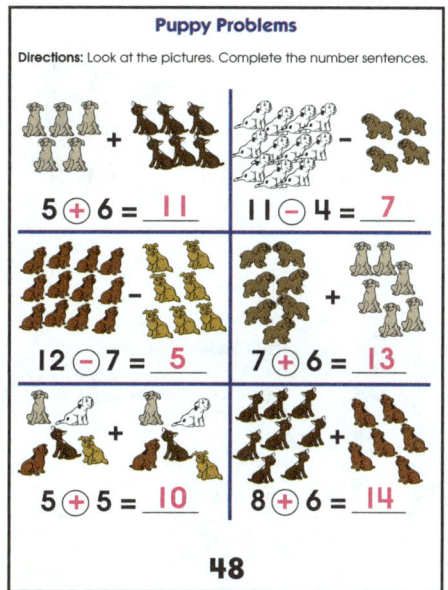

Puppy Problems

Directions: Look at the pictures. Complete the number sentences.

$$5 + 6 = 11$$
$$11 - 4 = 7$$
$$12 - 7 = 5$$
$$7 + 6 = 13$$
$$5 + 5 = 10$$
$$8 + 6 = 14$$

48

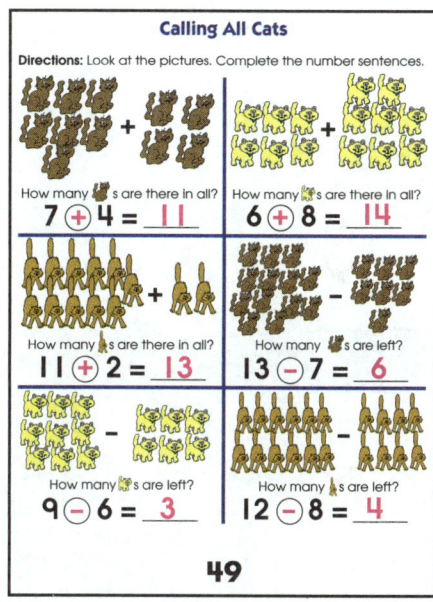

Calling All Cats

Directions: Look at the pictures. Complete the number sentences.

How many 🐱s are there in all?
$$7 + 4 = 11$$

How many 🐱s are there in all?
$$6 + 8 = 14$$

How many 🐱s are there in all?
$$11 + 2 = 13$$

How many 🐱s are left?
$$13 - 7 = 6$$

How many 🐱s are left?
$$9 - 6 = 3$$

How many 🐱s are left?
$$12 - 8 = 4$$

49

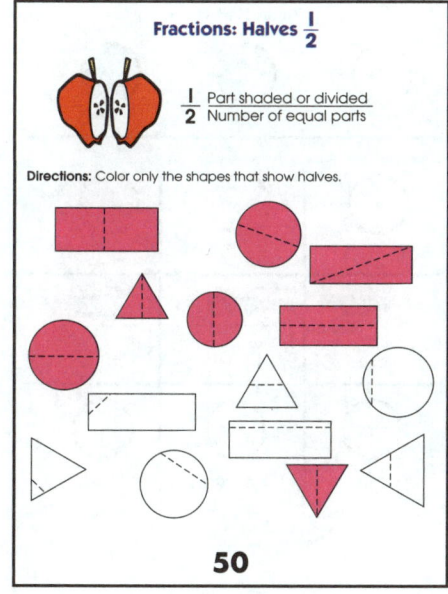

Fractions: Halves $\frac{1}{2}$

$\frac{1}{2}$ Part shaded or divided / Number of equal parts

Directions: Color only the shapes that show halves.

50

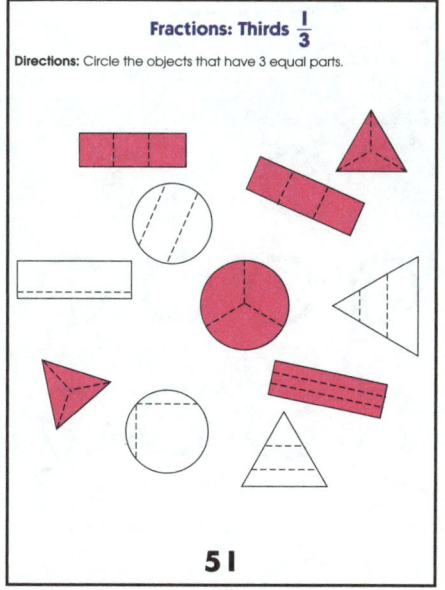

Fractions: Thirds $\frac{1}{3}$

Directions: Circle the objects that have 3 equal parts.

51

Math: Grade 1

Fractions: Fourths $\frac{1}{4}$

Directions: Circle the objects that have 4 equal parts.

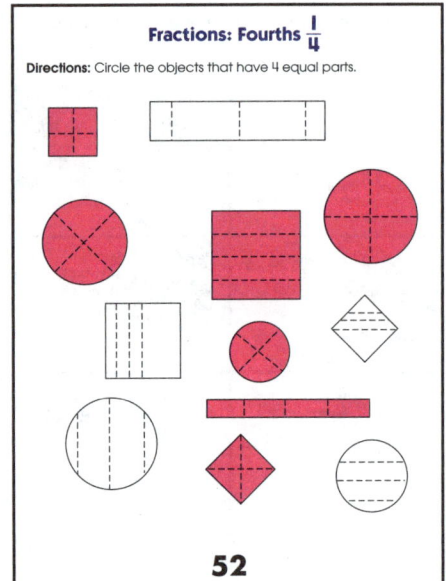

Fractions: Thirds and Fourths

Directions: Each object has 3 equal parts. Color one section.

Directions: Each object has 4 equal parts. Color one section.

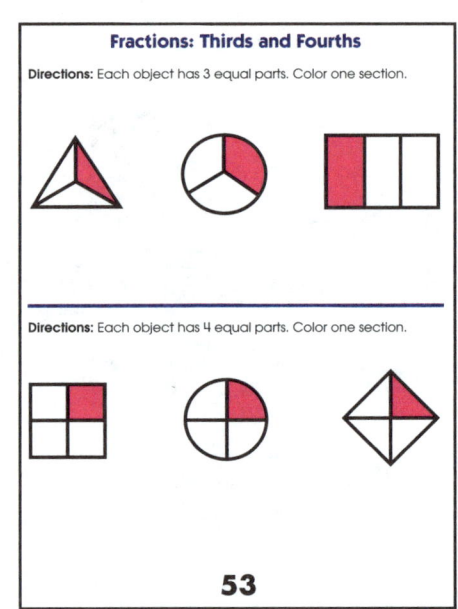

52

53

Review: Fractions

Directions: Count the equal parts. Then, write the fraction.

Example:

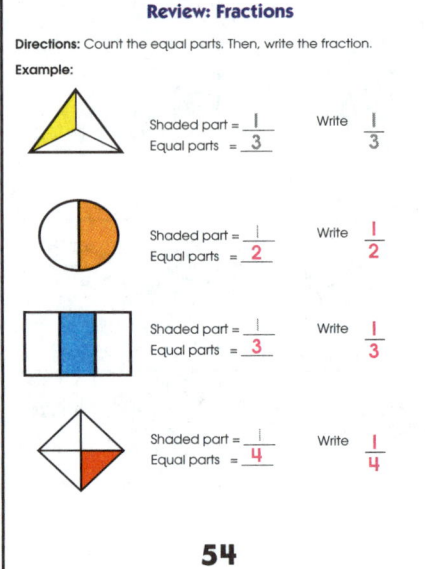

Shaded part = $\underline{1}$ Write $\frac{1}{3}$
Equal parts = $\underline{3}$

Shaded part = $\underline{1}$ Write $\frac{1}{2}$
Equal parts = $\underline{2}$

Shaded part = $\underline{1}$ Write $\frac{1}{3}$
Equal parts = $\underline{3}$

Shaded part = $\underline{1}$ Write $\frac{1}{4}$
Equal parts = $\underline{4}$

54

Fractions

The monsters are studying the moon. It changes its appearance as the month goes by. Sometimes the full moon is seen. Sometimes only part of it is seen. When only part of the moon is showing, it is a **fraction** of its full size.

Directions: Help the monsters learn fractions by filling in the blanks below.

Pretend the moon is divided into 2 equal parts.

$\frac{2}{2}$ The moon is full. The monsters see both of its 2 parts.

$\frac{1}{2}$ This is a half moon. The monsters see only $\underline{1}$ of its 2 parts.

What if you divided the moon into 4 equal parts?

$\frac{4}{4}$ The moon is full. The monsters can see all 4 of its $\underline{4}$ parts.

$\frac{3}{4}$ The moon is almost full. The monsters can see $\underline{3}$ of the 4 parts.

$\frac{2}{4}$ The moon is half full. The monsters can see $\underline{2}$ of the 4 parts.

$\frac{1}{4}$ The moon is almost gone. Only $\underline{1}$ part is left.

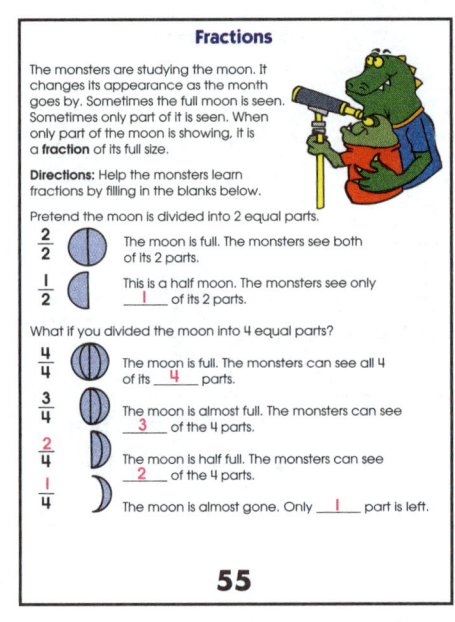

55

Time: Hour

The short hand of the clock tells the hour. The long hand tells how many minutes after the hour. When the minute hand is on the **12**, it is the beginning of the hour.

Directions: Look at each clock. Write the time.

Example:

$\underline{3}$ o'clock

$\underline{9}$ o'clock $\underline{1}$ o'clock $\underline{8}$ o'clock $\underline{11}$ o'clock

$\underline{5}$ o'clock $\underline{2}$ o'clock $\underline{10}$ o'clock $\underline{12}$ o'clock

56

Time: Hour, Half-Hour

The little hand of the clock tells the hour. The big hand tells how many minutes after the hour. When the minute hand is on the **6**, it is on the half-hour. A half-hour is thirty minutes. It is written **:30**, such as **5:30**.

Directions: Look at each clock. Write the time.

Example:

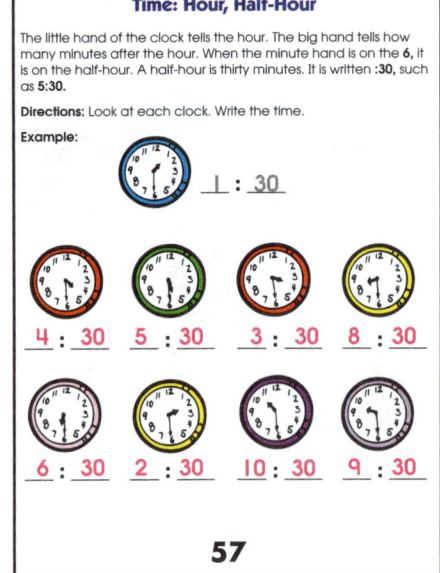

$\underline{1} : \underline{30}$

$\underline{4} : \underline{30}$ $\underline{5} : \underline{30}$ $\underline{3} : \underline{30}$ $\underline{8} : \underline{30}$

$\underline{6} : \underline{30}$ $\underline{2} : \underline{30}$ $\underline{10} : \underline{30}$ $\underline{9} : \underline{30}$

57

Time: Half-Hour

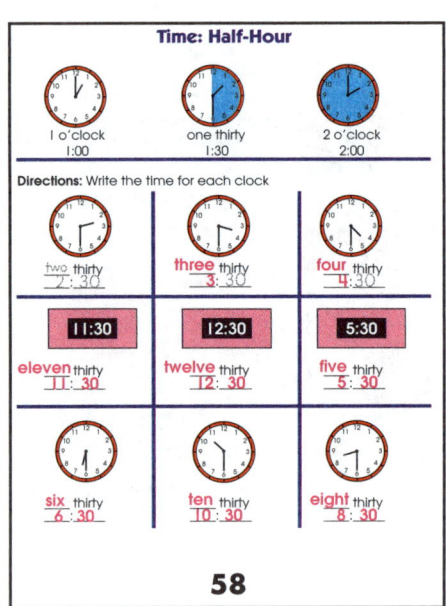

1 o'clock   one thirty   2 o'clock
1:00   1:30   2:00

Directions: Write the time for each clock

two thirty   three thirty   four thirty
$\underline{2} : \underline{30}$ $\underline{3} : \underline{30}$ $\underline{4} : \underline{30}$

| 11:30 | 12:30 | 5:30 |

eleven thirty   twelve thirty   five thirty
$\underline{11} : \underline{30}$ $\underline{12} : \underline{30}$ $\underline{5} : \underline{30}$

six thirty   ten thirty   eight thirty
$\underline{6} : \underline{30}$ $\underline{10} : \underline{30}$ $\underline{8} : \underline{30}$

58

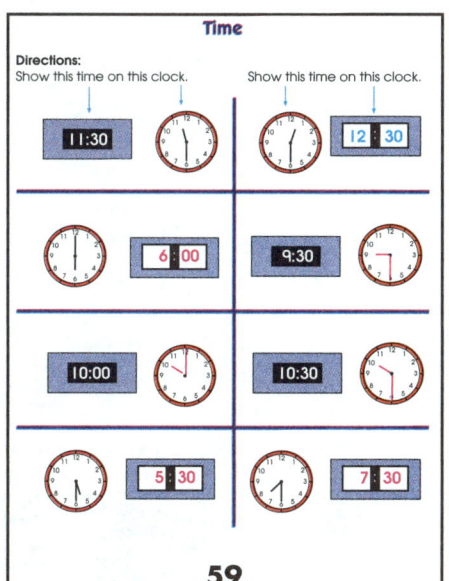

Time

Directions:
Show this time on this clock.

Show this time on this clock.

11:30

12:30

6:00

9:30

10:00

10:30

5:30

7:30

59

Time

The **little hand** on a clock points to the **hour**. The **big hand** points to the minutes. When the big hand reaches **12**, a new hour begins.

Directions: Look at all the things Juan is doing today. Write the number that tells the time of each activity. The first one is done for you.

It is _6_ o'clock.

It is _8_ o'clock.

It is _9_ o'clock.

It is _5_ o'clock.

It is _7_ o'clock.

It is _10_ o'clock.

60

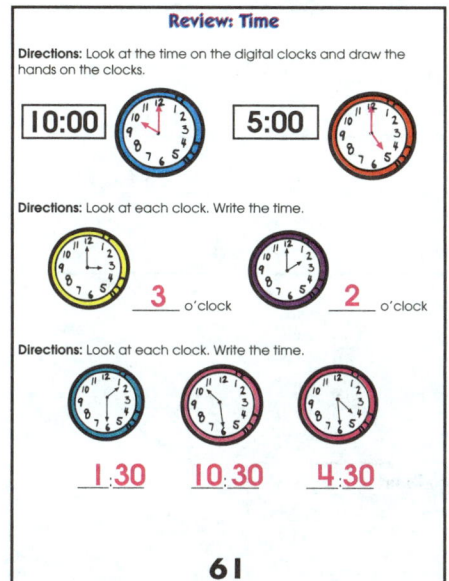

Review: Time

Directions: Look at the time on the digital clocks and draw the hands on the clocks.

10:00

5:00

Directions: Look at each clock. Write the time.

_3_ o'clock

_2_ o'clock

Directions: Look at each clock. Write the time.

_1:30_

_10:30_

_4:30_

61

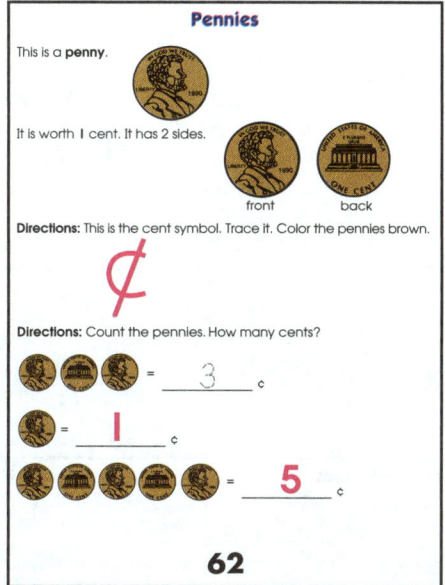

Pennies

This is a **penny**.

It is worth 1 cent. It has 2 sides.

front   back

Directions: This is the cent symbol. Trace it. Color the pennies brown.

¢

Directions: Count the pennies. How many cents?

= _3_ ¢

= _1_ ¢

= _5_ ¢

62

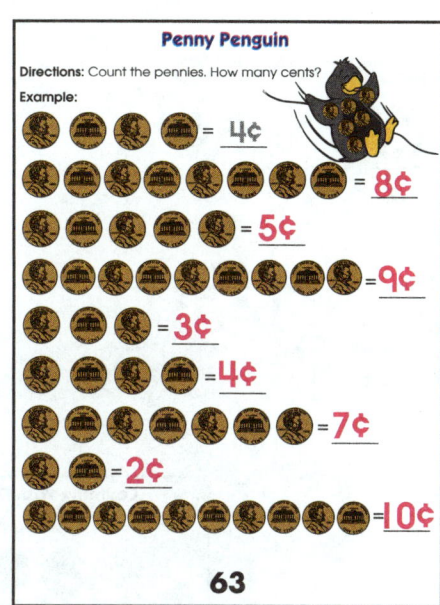

Penny Penguin

Directions: Count the pennies. How many cents?
Example:

= _4¢_

= _8¢_

= _5¢_

= _9¢_

= _3¢_

= _4¢_

= _7¢_

= _2¢_

= _10¢_

63

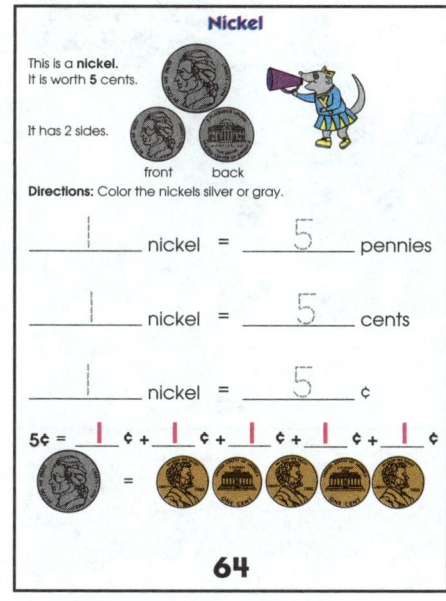

Nickel

This is a **nickel**.
It is worth **5 cents**.

It has 2 sides.

front   back

Directions: Color the nickels silver or gray.

_1_ nickel = _5_ pennies

_1_ nickel = _5_ cents

_1_ nickel = _5_ ¢

5¢ = _1_ ¢ + _1_ ¢ + _1_ ¢ + _1_ ¢ + _1_ ¢

=

64

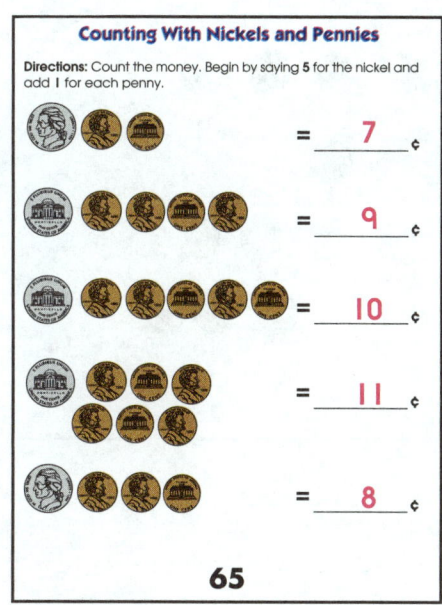

Counting With Nickels and Pennies

Directions: Count the money. Begin by saying **5** for the nickel and add **1** for each penny.

= _7_ ¢

= _9_ ¢

= _10_ ¢

= _11_ ¢

= _8_ ¢

65

Adding With Nick and Penny

Directions: Write how much money there is in all.

PENNY

`3` ¢
`+` `3` ¢
`6` ¢ in all

`5` ¢ `+` `5` ¢ `=` `10` in all

NICK

`7` ¢
`+` `7` ¢
`14` ¢ in all

66

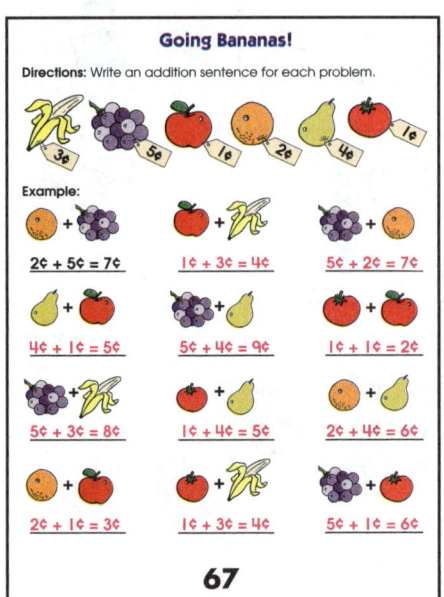

Going Bananas!

Directions: Write an addition sentence for each problem.

3¢ 5¢ 1¢ 2¢ 4¢ 1¢

Example:

2¢ + 5¢ = 7¢   1¢ + 3¢ = 4¢   5¢ + 2¢ = 7¢

4¢ + 1¢ = 5¢   5¢ + 4¢ = 9¢   1¢ + 1¢ = 2¢

5¢ + 3¢ = 8¢   1¢ + 4¢ = 5¢   2¢ + 4¢ = 6¢

2¢ + 1¢ = 3¢   1¢ + 3¢ = 4¢   5¢ + 1¢ = 6¢

67

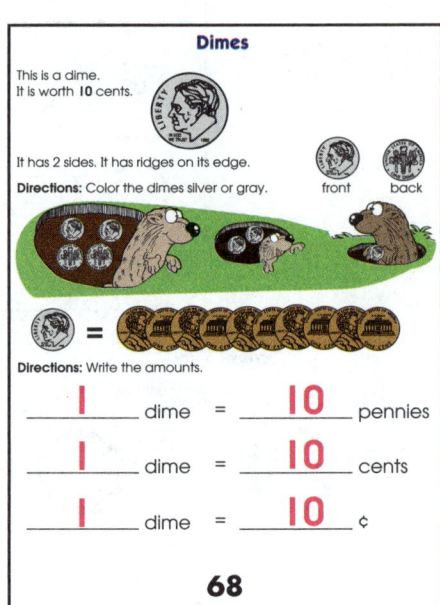

Dimes

This is a dime.
It is worth 10 cents.

It has 2 sides. It has ridges on its edge.

Directions: Color the dimes silver or gray.

front   back

=

Directions: Write the amounts.

`1` dime = `10` pennies

`1` dime = `10` cents

`1` dime = `10` ¢

68

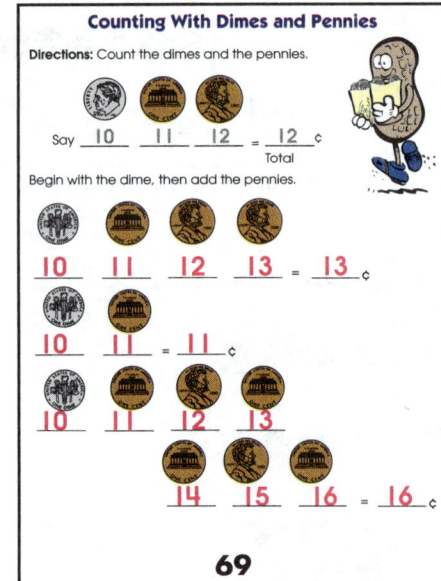

Counting With Dimes and Pennies

Directions: Count the dimes and the pennies.

Say `10` `11` `12` = `12` ¢
Total

Begin with the dime, then add the pennies.

`10` `11` `12` `13` = `13` ¢

`10` `11` = `11` ¢

`10` `11` `12` `13`

`14` `15` `16` = `16` ¢

69

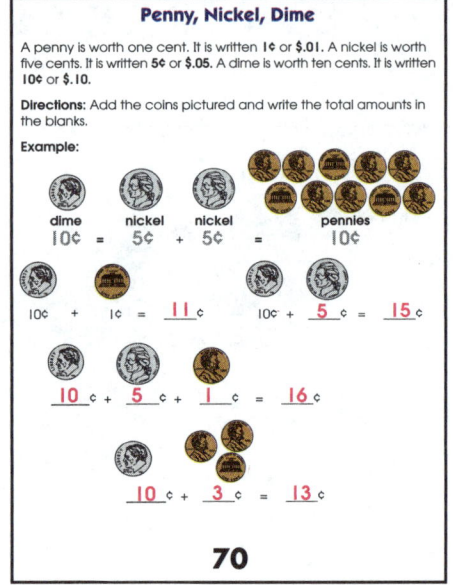

Penny, Nickel, Dime

A penny is worth one cent. It is written 1¢ or $.01. A nickel is worth five cents. It is written 5¢ or $.05. A dime is worth ten cents. It is written 10¢ or $.10.

Directions: Add the coins pictured and write the total amounts in the blanks.

Example:

dime   nickel   nickel   pennies
10¢ = 5¢ + 5¢ = 10¢

10¢ + 1¢ = `11` ¢   10¢ + `5` ¢ = `15` ¢

`10` ¢ + `5` ¢ + `1` ¢ = `16` ¢

`10` ¢ + `3` ¢ = `13` ¢

70